THE UPPER ROOM

DAILY MEDITATIONS FROM AROUND THE WORLD

Sarah Wilke
Publisher

Fotis Romeos
Guest Editor

INTERDENOMINATIONAL
INTERNATIONAL
INTERRACIAL

80 EDITIONS
40 LANGUAGES

The Upper Room
May–August 2011
Edited by Susan Hibbins

The Upper Room © BRF 2011
The Bible Reading Fellowship
15 The Chambers, Vineyard, Abingdon OX14 3FE
Tel: 01865 319700; Fax: 01865 319701
Email: enquiries@brf.org.uk
Website: www.brf.org.uk
BRF is a Registered Charity

ISBN 978 1 84101 792 1

Acknowledgments

Printed in the UK by HSW Print.

The Upper Room: how to use this book

The Upper Room is ideal in helping us spend a quiet time with God each day. Each daily entry is based on a passage of scripture, and is followed by a meditation and prayer. Each person who contributes a meditation to the magazine seeks to relate their experience of God in a way that will help those who use *The Upper Room* every day.

Here are some guidelines to help you make best use of *The Upper Room*:

1. Read the passage of scripture. It is a good idea to read it more than once, in order to have a fuller understanding of what it is about and what you can learn from it.
2. Read the meditation. How does it relate to your own experience? Can you identify with what the writer has outlined from their own experience or understanding?
3. Pray the written prayer. Think about how you can use it to relate to people you know, or situations that need your prayers today.
4. Think about the contributor who has written the meditation. Some Upper Room users include this person in their prayers for the day.
5. Meditate on the 'Thought for the day', the 'Link2Life' and the 'Prayer Focus', perhaps using them again as the focus for prayer or direction for action.

Why is it important to have a daily quiet time? Many people will agree that it is the best way of keeping in touch every day with the God who sustains us, and who sends us out to do his will and show his love to the people we encounter each day. Meeting with God in this way reassures us of his presence with us, helps us to discern his will for us and makes us part of his worldwide family of Christian people through our prayers.

I hope that you will be encouraged as you use the magazine regularly as part of your daily devotions, and that God will richly bless you as you read his word and seek to learn more about him.

Susan Hibbins
UK Editor

In Times of/For Help with . . .

Below is a list of entries in this copy of *The Upper Room* relating to situations or emotions with which we may need help:

Anger: Aug 10, 24

Anxiety: July 9, 24, 30; Aug 9, 19

Bible reading: May 2, 3, 7, 12, 28, 30; July 8, 14, 16, 22, 28; Aug 13

Change: July 21; Aug 8, 11, 21

Christian community: May 2, 11, 20, 30; June 1, 4, 12; July 12, 30; Aug 2, 4, 11

Compassion: May 5, 12, 26, 30, 31; June 6; July 10, 14, 23, 30; Aug 14

Conflict: May 13, 16

Creation/nature: May 13, 14, 17; June 1, 15, 17; July 5, 6, 17; Aug 9, 16, 25

Death/grief: May 8, 12, 26; June 5, 19; July 2, 11; Aug 6

Evangelism: May 11, 15, 22, 25, 27; June 9, 11, 12, 19, 23; July 10, 26; Aug 16

Failure: July 6, 18; Aug 10, 26

Family: May 4, 6, 8, 14, 16; June 1, 9; July 2, 7; Aug 6, 10, 12, 14

Fear: July 9, 13, 24, 31; Aug 4, 19

Financial concerns: July 21; Aug 3, 11

Forgiveness: May 1, 11, 31; June 8, 25, 28; July 13; Aug 24, 26, 27

Friendship: July 12, 30; Aug 17, 24

Generosity/giving: May 22, 27, 31; June 17, 22, 26; July 10; Aug 3, 9, 20

God's comfort: May 12, 18, 26; June 14

God's love: May 4, 16, 21; June 7, 14, 21, 28; July 5, 7, 19, 30; Aug 1, 9, 12

God's power: July 9, 13, 24; Aug 25

God's presence: May 26; June 2, 12, 14; July 6, 19, 31; Aug 14, 18, 30

God's provision: May 22, 29; June 17, 24; July 13, 15, 30; Aug 17, 19, 20

God's will: July 15, 22

Gratitude: May 31; June 19; Aug 22

Growth: May 7, 16, 24; June 4, 5, 12, 29; July 3, 11, 21; Aug 5, 8, 10, 25

Guidance: May 17, 25, 28, 31; July 15, 22, 27; Aug 15

Healing/illness: May 8, 14, 18; June 8, 14; July 3, 14, 20, 24, 25, 30; Aug 11, 17

Hope/future: July 21; Aug 9, 10

Hospitality: Aug 2, 3

Job issues: May 29; June 24; July 9; Aug 1

Judging: May 10, 16, 19; June 4, 9

Living our faith: May 5, 15; June 3, 6, 9, 22, 27; July 2, 16, 23; Aug 2, 3, 16

Loss: May 8, 12, 14, 18, 29; June 3, 5, 18; July 11, 21; Aug 6

Materialism: May 3, 15, 27, 28; June 11, 17, 22, 26; Aug 11, 25

New beginnings: July 18, 25; Aug 26

Obedience: May 28, 30, 31; June 6, 10, 12, 22, 27; July 27, 29; Aug 15, 27

Parenting: May 4, 21, 24, 28; June 10, 13, 19, 20; July 2, 7, 23, 25; Aug 10, 30

Peace/unrest: July 19, 31; Aug 7, 10

Prayer: May 5, 8, 14, 21; June 1, 29; July 1, 28, 31; Aug 2, 7, 9, 31

Prison ministry: July 1, 18

Repentance/sin: July 6, 12, 18; Aug 26

Salvation: July 12, 18, 25; Aug 24

Serving: May 5, 11, 15, 19, 25, 30, 31; June 1, 11; July 14, 17, 20, 23, 25, 30

Social issues: May 13, 20, 22; June 3, 10, 16; Aug 10, 29

Spiritual practices: May 2, 3, 9, 22; June 1, 30; July 2, 8, 28; Aug 1, 5, 7, 13

Stewardship: May 25; June 1, 26; Aug 9

Stress: May 7, 17; June 2, 7, 10; July 1, 3, 21; Aug 1, 3, 5, 7, 8, 11, 15

Temptation: May 3, 17, 28

Trouble/challenge: July 6, 9; Aug 4, 13

Trust: May 18, 29; June 2, 10, 24; July 13, 29; Aug 4, 15, 18, 28

Power to be witnesses

'You will receive power when the Holy Spirit has come upon you; and you will be my witnesses in Jerusalem, in all Judea and Samaria, and to the ends of the earth' (Acts 1:8, NRSV).

In Greece where I live, we have not only thousands of years of political history but also a long history of the presence of Christ's Church. And just as we Greeks take for granted our ethnic heritage, we often take for granted the presence of the gospel in our region.

For some, Greece has become only a nominally Christian nation. Many might say we Greeks need to rediscover the presence of God, the power of the gospel and the reality of the Holy Spirit.

Jesus' commission to his disciples before his ascension that they become his witnesses is still valid for us today. Our nation has a wonderful religious tradition, tremendous theological writings and a historic ecclesiastic structure. But we need living witnesses of Jesus Christ in our everyday life. Genuine Christian witnesses are those who have experienced the life of Christ, are ready to express his message in their everyday actions and are willing to reach out to meet the needs of the people with his loving compassion during these critical times.

Last year we celebrated the 75th anniversary of Upper Room ministries here in Greece along with our partners all over the world. My prayer is that we may all experience anew in this generation the power of the Holy Spirit that came on the original 'upper room' many years ago. The living Christ is available to us and to all the world. Let us each carry the torch of the gospel witness of Jesus: 'to the ends of the earth'.

Let's become authentic witnesses of Christ until he comes again!

Rev. Fotis Romeos
Editor, Epiousious Artos (Daily Bread) (The Upper Room's Greek edition)

This guest editorial is the third in a series as we celebrate *The Upper Room*'s reach into more than 100 countries.

The Editor writes...

I wonder if you have watched the BBC TV programme called *Restoration*. In a slightly different twist on the usual antique valuation programmes, people brought along items that had been languishing in lofts or garages, suffering from serious neglect. A battered rocking horse, its paint worn away and runners broken, gazed sadly at a three-legged, scratched table, while a china shepherdess looked out at them both from beneath her chipped and cracked summer hat. All of them looked beyond repair, and yet, in the hands of expert restorers, the rocking horse was ready to race again, the table stood upright on four legs, and the shepherdess had a brand new hat. It was impossible to see where the restoration work began or ended.

It was especially fascinating to see the experts working on a painting. Years of grime were stripped away, and fire or water damage was repaired to reveal fresh and vibrant colours that could not even be seen before. All the time the restorer worked patiently to reveal what he or she knew lay hidden, until the painting looked as it had done the day that the artist had completed it.

We may feel that sometimes we are in need of restoration. Life leaves its mark on us too, and we can feel battered and worn. Our best intentions are often obscured by the problems of daily living; bits of us are damaged, maybe, we feel, beyond repair. The good news is that we have a Master Restorer who, when he looks at us, sees what his original creation will become, despite all our current imperfections. He knows that, although we might be a 'work in progress', one day we will stand, perfected. And our Master Restorer has all of this life and the next to complete his work.

Susan Hibbins
Editor of the UK edition

PS: The Bible readings are selected with great care, and we urge you to include the suggested reading in your devotional time.

Settle Up Sooner

Read Matthew 5:21–25
Do two walk together unless they have agreed to do so?
Amos 3:3 (NIV)

Sometimes when I'm walking to warm up before I run, I get a small pebble in my shoe. At first I simply ignore it, but the more I do, the bigger the pebble seems to become. When I can't stand it any longer and the pebble feels as if it has grown into a stone, I stop and empty my shoe. I think to myself, 'Why I did I wait so long to empty my shoe and get rid of the pain?'

This reminds me of the advice Jesus gives us in Matthew 5:25 to 'settle matters quickly' when we are at odds with another person. Whatever has occurred between us and a friend to upset us will not change. It only seems to grow and get worse the longer we wait. But when we settle our differences sooner, we save ourselves the unnecessary suffering.

Prayer: *Dear Lord, give us the wisdom and the willingness to say we are sorry sooner rather than later. In Jesus' name we pray. Amen*

Thought for the day: Whether we are asking forgiveness or offering it, God is pleased.

Tom Hite (Virginia, US)

Companions for the Journey

Read Ecclesiastes 4:9–12

Where two or three come together in my name, there am I with them.
Matthew 18:20 (NIV)

I was brought up in a Christian home, but my family did not regularly attend church. After college, I returned to my home town, but many of my friends had moved away. I felt lonely and disconnected, so I began to look for a church in order to meet new people. I started attending and was asked to join a small-group Bible study. At first I felt apprehensive because I did not know anyone in the group. But through God's gentle prodding, I accepted the invitation and began to go to the study. It was a life-changing experience.

Through the study, I learned to care for other people in a deeper way. The group members supported one another. We carried each other through many of life's hard times, and we shared in each other's joys. The small group was my lifeline and support for many years.

Through this experience, I realised that God does not intend for us to walk through life alone. God demonstrates love for us through the Christian friends in our lives. God gives us to one another to lean on each other, support each other, teach each other and, mostly importantly, love each other.

Prayer: *Source of all true joy, thank you for our Christian family and for the love and support they share with us. In Jesus' name. Amen*

Thought for the day: Who are the special people God has placed in my life?

Link2Life: *Start a small Bible study group.*

Sheri Rea (Pennsylvania, US)

Spiritual Weed Killer

Read Matthew 13:1–9, 18–23

[God's] divine power has given us everything we need for life and godliness through our knowledge of him who called us by his own glory and goodness.
2 Peter 1:3 (NIV)

I had been busy, distracted and forgetful. The real problem, however, was my lack of effort. The garden was overrun with weeds. Shrubs were dying and flowers were smothered. While I had once taken pride in my garden, I now felt ashamed of it. Restoring it would require much personal effort and significant cost.

As I surveyed the scene, its spiritual implications became clear in my mind. Jesus had warned about this very thing. The parable of the sower in the gospels reveals what happens to our faith when we fail to protect God's word in our inner being. Life's worries, the deceitfulness of riches and the lure of pleasures can combine to suffocate spirituality. We cannot escape their 'seeds'. However, we can prevent them from taking root in us.

Our Lord has provided resources in scripture for us to deal with moral and spiritual 'weeds'. I especially like the ones promoted by 2 Peter 1:5–7. 'Faith, goodness, perseverance, godliness and love' blend to protect our spiritual health and well-being.

Prayer: *Dear Lord, thank you for your provision for our total well-being. May we be faithful in applying these spiritual resources to our life. Amen*

Thought for the day: With God's help, we can displace weeds with healthy growth.

Link2Life: *Volunteer in or set up a community garden.*

Raymond N. Hawkins (Tasmania, Australia)

Timely Words

Read Psalm 139:13–18

I praise you because I am fearfully and wonderfully made; your works are wonderful, I know that full well.

Psalm 139:14 (NIV)

My grandfather was a man of few words. The deep lines on his face and hands told of his many years of service in the navy and the local fire department, and somewhere along this difficult journey, my grandfather had developed mastery of the timely word. My brother and I knew the signs—when we saw his twinkling glance and the thin curve of his smile, we would wait in suspense for his perfect joke.

As Grandfather's health began to fail last year, he turned that careful expressiveness to the messages of love he wanted to leave. My mother weeps openly when she recounts how the former seaman gazed at her with eyes deep as the oceans he once sailed and said to her, 'I love you.' At the end of a life full of timely words, his last was to let his child know how special she was to him.

In the Bible, we can read that the psalmist understood that God sees each of us the same way Grandfather saw his daughter, as a beloved child. Each of us is 'fearfully and wonderfully made', the pinnacle of God's creation. I will take comfort in the assurance of our Creator's skilful handiwork and his great love for each one of us.

Prayer: *Loving God, thank you for making us part of your creation. Help us to see others and ourselves as you do. Amen*

Thought for the day: God looks at each of us through eyes filled with love.

Derik Timmerman (North Carolina, US)

PRAYER FOCUS: THOSE WHO FEEL UNLOVED

Paying Attention

Read Romans 12:9–15
Let each of you look not to your own interests, but to the interests of others.
Philippians 2:4 (NRSV)

Hushed sobs came from the room outside my office. A woman cried as she talked on the phone about her marital problems. 'Should I go to her?' I wondered. 'No, she needs her privacy.' But the heartbreak in her voice pulled at me. Later, I gently approached her, asking if I could do anything to help. She told me some of her story, and we prayed. In the days that followed I couldn't forget about our encounter, and I prayed for the woman often. I was touched by the few moments we had spent together.

A week later, the woman came looking for me. Her desolation of the week before was replaced with an ear-to-ear smile. She gave me a tight hug, thanked me for praying with her and told me things were much better.

I always feel good when God uses me to help another person. But what if I had stayed so wrapped up in my own work or worries that I had not noticed her crying? Sometimes, the first step is simply to listen, to close the laptop, to turn off the mobile phone, to put down the book and to pay attention. We may be humbled and blessed by what God can do when we listen and respond to what we hear.

Prayer: *Dear God, use us to help others. Amen*

Thought for the day: I will listen to the cries of those in need.

Link2Life: *Find out the needs of those near you and pray for them.*

Janis Meredith (California, US)

A Witness for the Spirit

Read 1 Corinthians 11:23–26

[Jesus] said: 'I tell you the truth, unless you change and become like little children, you will never enter the kingdom of heaven.'
Matthew 18:3 (NIV)

Stian came from Sunday school to the sanctuary just in time for Holy Communion. I knelt at the altar rail next to him. He had brought a drawing he'd made in class; so he looked at me and whispered: 'I need to put it here on the floor because there will be so much in my hands when the minister comes to me.'

As he received the bread, I could hear him chew; he made small noises that showed he enjoyed the taste. He received the small cup and slurped the liquid down, making sure he got it all before he handed the cup back.

Stian is only six years old. He knows, perhaps intuitively, that he needs to stretch out two empty hands to receive Jesus. His whole body made clear that it was good to be close to Christ through Communion. With a child's understanding, he witnessed that the body and blood of Christ are life-giving.

For me, this incident became a holy moment, the child at my side a witness for the Holy Spirit. With the attitude and openness of a child, I can fully receive the love of God.

Prayer: *Loving God, help us to be like children who are open to your love, without second thoughts or doubts. Strengthen our trust in you as your beloved children. Amen*

Thought for the day: God fills our empty hands with love.

Link2Life: *Choose a child you know and pray for that child by name every day.*

Wenche Moe Aasmundtveit (Vestfold, Norway)

In a Scorched Land

Read John 4:5–15

The Lord will guide you always; he will satisfy your needs in a sun-scorched land and will strengthen your frame. You will be like a well-watered garden, like a spring whose waters never fail.
Isaiah 58:11 (NIV)

I was parched with thirst, and my head hurt. It was day three of a four-day hiking and backpacking excursion in the Appalachian Mountains. Our adventurous group—four trail guides, three adults and six teenagers—had just reached a mountaintop, stopping for a brief rest before continuing our journey. As I sat on a rock to rest, I gulped my last drops of water and some of a friend's as well. Slowly, my headache eased, and the heat didn't feel quite so intense.

On this trip we all came to appreciate water as never before. Before beginning each day's hike we filled two water bottles apiece, carefully storing them in our packs. Running out of water could spell dehydration and danger in the middle of the wilderness, so we kept ourselves well supplied.

Spiritually, I have often felt the need for refreshment in the midst of an intense situation or season of life. Feeling drained of strength, I might have given up during those times. But by turning to the life-giving word of God for refreshment, I have been sustained and fuelled to continue my walk of faith. Every day we need spiritual water, and every day God offers it.

Prayer: *Dear Lord, we turn to you for refreshment. Your wisdom will forever guide us, and we will always find true rest in you. Amen*

Thought for the day: God offers us spiritual refreshment even in scorched places.

Melissa S. Chappell (North Carolina, US)

Waiting with Others

Read Psalm 5:1–12

In the morning I lay my requests before you [O Lord] and wait in expectation.
Psalm 5:3 (NIV)

My mother is in the last stages of her battle with cancer. Each day that I have with her is a gift from God. Some days are better than others; and sometimes, in beautiful moments, we connect and have a great talk. After these times I am glad that I was there, sitting with her and caring for her.

The special moments with my mother have reminded me to take the time to sit with the Lord, in anticipation of God's speaking to me. God may not speak to me every day or every week; but unless I am listening, I will never hear what God wants to say.

My mother will be leaving me soon, sooner than I would like; but the Lord will never leave me. Despite this time of sad farewells, I have treasured being with my mum and with my Lord. God is truly the Lord of peace and love, and I am thankful to wait in God's presence and to connect with God and with the people I love.

Prayer: *Thank you, God, for each day and each moment we spend with those we love and with you. Thank you for loving us and caring for us at all times. Thank you for your peace that surpasses understanding. As Jesus taught us, we pray, 'Our Father in heaven, hallowed be your name, your kingdom come, your will be done on earth as it is in heaven. Give us today our daily bread. Forgive us our debts, as we also have forgiven our debtors. And lead us not into temptation, but deliver us from the evil one.'* Amen*

Thought for the day: When we listen, we will hear God speak.

Melora Hirschman (Nebraska, US)

PRAYER FOCUS: THOSE WAITING AT THE BEDSIDE OF SOMEONE THEY LOVE
* Matthew 6:9–13 (NIV)

The Ready Room

Read 1 Corinthians 6:12–14, 19–20

Whatever is true… honourable… just… pure… pleasing… commendable, if there is any excellence and if there is anything worthy of praise, think about these things.

Philippians 4:8 (NRSV)

My house has a guest room, but it has become a storeroom. The bed is covered with clutter, and my junk occupies every level surface. If I should have a guest, the bed would not be ready, and the guest would have no room to set out their belongings.

I think my spirit often tends to be like that guest room. Day by day, it's easy to allow my spirit to fill with thoughts and influences that simply don't leave much room for God. The antidote is to keep it clean and clear.

We might consider some distractions benign and some resentments natural, but they use space that God could fill with healthy thoughts, wise counsel and love. Those derive from time with God when our spirits are well prepared.

This guest-room analogy helps me to understand more about maintaining a right relationship with God, but the comparison is flawed. God should not be considered a guest; God is master. The small guest room is not for God to visit occasionally; the entire house is God's to occupy perpetually. And, I honour God by keeping it ready and welcoming.

Prayer: *O God, help us to empty our baggage and make uncluttered space in our spirits for you. Amen*

Thought for the day: How can I prepare to welcome God into my days?

Kenneth Athon (Indiana, US)

Hidden Treasures

Read James 2:1–13

Peter began to speak to [those gathered at the house of Cornelius]: 'I truly understand that God shows no partiality.'
Acts 10:34 (NRSV)

Two years ago I was given a nondescript plant. I was told it would be beautiful, with blooms that opened up late in the day and closed at sunset. Weeks later, I noticed a pleasant fragrance wafting through the house. I rushed to the balcony to see that a beautiful bloom had sprouted on the plant.

In a similar way, the world discovered Susan Boyle, a middle-aged, Scottish woman. Simply dressed and without make-up, she crossed a stage to debut before a demanding panel of judges on a popular TV show in England. At first, the audience and judges' reaction was sceptical, at best. How great was their astonishment when she began to sing! At the end of the performance she received a standing ovation. Like us in many situations, the audience had judged Susan by her outer appearance.

The plant and Susan's story remind us to leave all judgment to God. We get insight into the nature of God's judgment in his words to Samuel about David's brother Eliab: 'Do not look on his appearance or the height of his stature, because I have rejected him; for the Lord does not see as mortals see; they look on the outward appearance, but the Lord looks on the heart' (1 Samuel 16:7).

Prayer: *Dear God of love, help us to see other people the way you do.*

Thought for the day: When we see others through God's eyes, we see their true worth.

Link2Life: *Watch Susan Boyle's performance on YouTube.*

Esperanza C. Acosta Núñez (National District, Dominican Republic)

You are the Message

Read Matthew 11:1–6

Let your light shine before others, so that they may see your good works and give glory to your Father in heaven.
Matthew 5:16 (NRSV)

When my family first moved to the area where we now live, we attended a small church. We found that the pastor was highly respected and admired. I asked a neighbour why this was. 'Well,' he replied, 'his life and his words match. He teaches a lot about love, and he lives the love.'

The Bible offers us Jesus as the ultimate example of one whose words and life match. When John the Baptist was in prison, he sent some friends to ask Jesus if he was the 'one who was to come'. Jesus replied, 'Go back and report to John what you hear and see: The blind receive sight, the lame walk, those who have leprosy are cured, the deaf hear, the dead are raised, and the good news is preached to the poor' (Matthew 11:3–5, NIV). Like Jesus, our pastor lived what he taught.

You and I may be the only message of God's love, grace and forgiveness that many people hear and see. Are we living in ways that will lead others to believe and to 'praise [our] Father in heaven'?

Prayer: *All-powerful God, help us to make our words and actions match, to bring glory to you in all that we say and do. Amen*

Thought for the day: When we follow Jesus faithfully, our words and actions will match.

Bob Waymire (California, US)

God Understands

Read John 11:17–44

[God] will wipe every tear from their eyes. There will be no more death or mourning or crying or pain.
Revelation 21:4 (NIV)

A few years ago I was part of a discussion about favourite Bible verses. A colleague said that her favourite Bible verse was John 11:35. I did not know the verse from memory. When I had a chance to look it up, I was surprised to find which one it was. It's the shortest verse in the Bible. In fact, it's just two words: 'Jesus wept.'

When I asked my friend why she had picked that particular verse, she told me that this verse shows her the human side of Jesus. I knew that she had encountered much sorrow in her life. She said that there were times in life when she needed to cry, and she knows that Jesus could relate to her tears because he himself cried. To her, Jesus was never more human than when he was in pain. Whenever she cries, she remembers that while Jesus also endured tears and pain, through him, we believers will all be raised to glory one day.

My colleague's words offered me a new perspective. We can take heart from knowing that God can relate to our pain and comfort us, but also from knowing that a day is coming when there will be no pain and no suffering.

Prayer: *O God, thank you for being with us when we suffer and for your gift of eternal life through Christ. Amen*

Thought for the day: When we cry, God shares our tears and our pain.

John D. Bown (Minnesota, US)

All Are One

Read Galatians 3:23–29

There is no longer Jew or Greek, there is no longer slave or free, there is no longer male and female; for all of you are one in Christ Jesus.
Galatians 3:28 (NRSV)

My wife and I enjoyed a recent holiday in New Zealand where we saw thousands of sheep and cows. What caught my eye were the paddocks shared by both types of animals. This caused me to reflect on the early settlement of America where cattle ranchers and sheep ranchers killed each other and animals over the mistaken belief that it is not possible for sheep and cattle to live on the same lands.

These battles may be over, but we still haven't solved the problems of humans living together. We allow political differences, tribal differences, religious differences, racial differences, gender differences and many other factors to divide us. How sad it is that we do not heed the words Paul wrote to the Galatians—that God does not value one person over another. That we are clothed in Christ is all that matters to God.

If all of us were to follow Christ's teaching fully, conflicts over our differences would disappear. I look forward to the time when the lamb will not only lie down with the calf but ultimately with the wolf and the lion (see Isaiah 11:6).

Prayer: *Guide of humanity, may your kingdom come and the battles among people be replaced with peace and understanding. Amen*

Thought for the day: Through Christ, peace is possible.

Jeral Williams (Alabama, US)

Broken Pieces

Read Psalm 147:1–14
[The Lord] heals the brokenhearted and binds up their wounds.
Psalm 147:3 (NIV)

One night my three-year-old granddaughter looked up at a bright crescent moon and said, 'Grandma, the moon is broken!' I explained to her that the moon moves into phases and that in a few weeks God would 'mend' it and once again we would see a full, 'unbroken' moon.

As we finished our walk, I began to reflect on my life of 80 years and remembered its broken pieces. My daughter, Marie, had suffered a near-fatal head-on car accident; Linda, my second daughter, endured an embolism that nearly ended her life. As I prayed, I was comforted with God's loving presence. I still sense God's nearness today as I care for my husband, who has suffered two strokes.

I have grown deeper in my faith because of the challenges I have faced. Through them I have come to realise that there is power in prayer, and I am comforted by the thought that God continues to heal the physical and the spiritual brokenness in our lives.

Prayer: *Thank you, Lord, that you are with us in every challenge we face. Amen*

Thought for the day: God is at work to mend the brokenness within us.

Audrey Kline (New York, US)

PRAYER FOCUS: THOSE RECOVERING AFTER A STROKE

So Many New Things!

Read Isaiah 43:16–21

Then the one who sits on the throne said, 'And now I make all things new!'
Revelation 21:5 (GNB)

One of my special pleasures at school was to be given a new note-book from the stationery cupboard. I would open it straight away to smell its pages, each one fresh, clean and blank, waiting for me to pick up my pencil and write. I still delight in new notebooks, or in new clothes or shoes—and most of all in every new day.

As dawn breaks over the hills I realise that a whole new un-spoiled, unlived day lies ahead. In the quietness before it begins I am reminded that each hour is God's gift, and that he is eagerly waiting to show me new things, perhaps in the world around me, or in the words of a friend who calls. Often, too, it will be in learning something new from the Bible, or a new insight about a change in my inner life which God wants me to make.

So many new things! God says to me, 'Do not cling to events of the past… Watch for the new thing I am going to do. It is happening already—you can see it now!' (Isaiah 43:18–19). God so carefully plans new things for us each day, and it's exciting to watch them unfold as we enter into them. An experience definitely not to be missed!

Prayer: *Lord, help us to let go of the past so that we can reach out to valuable new discoveries ahead, in company with you. Amen*

Thought for the day: The new things God is eager to show me and give me today.

Elaine Brown (Pitlochry, Scotland)

Hearing the Cheers

Read Zephaniah 3:14–20

The Lord, your God… will rejoice over you with gladness, he will renew you in his love; he will exult over you with loud singing.
Zephaniah 3:17 (NRSV)

My niece played in a basketball team at a local church. During a game that we attended, one of the fathers became upset about the officiating, as well as the performance of his daughter and the other players. He became increasingly vocal as the game progressed, and he eventually caused loud discussions with the other parents who were trying to calm him down. After the game, my wife expressed concern that our niece had been disturbed by the noise off court. The young girl responded, 'All I could hear was cheering!'

We encounter a lot of 'noise' as we try to live as God has called us to. Many voices scream that life is not fair or that we are doing everything wrong. As we follow God as faithfully as we know how, we, like my niece and like the Jews of Zephaniah's time, can learn to tune out negative voices and to listen to the voice of God, who loves us and always cheers us on.

Prayer: *Dear Lord, teach us to recognise and listen to your voice. May we hear you encouraging us as we follow your leading in our lives. Amen*

Thought for the day: Listen to the voice of God, who seeks our good and cheers us on.

Donald E. Lott (Georgia, US)

The Big Picture

Read Psalm 119:169–176
May your hand [O Lord] be ready to help me.
Psalm 119:173 (NIV)

As I was walking outside one bleak morning, I looked across from the hill I was climbing. Below me stretched a broad river valley. On the other side of the valley a wall of low clouds obscured the countryside; but rising above the clouds were the distant peaks of mountains, blue-purple and vivid against the pale sky.

Sometimes life is like the valley where everything is clearly visible. We can see where we are going and spot obstacles we need to avoid. Sometimes we reach the peaks of the mountains. At other times, our way is obscured. Knowing where we are headed is difficult, as if we were trying to find our way through low clouds or fog and can no longer see the path clearly. We cannot see the details. We may see the broad outlines of the path but not the potholes, loose stones or muddy patches. Although the final destination is clear, we're not sure what our next step should be.

No matter where life takes us or how obscured the path is, God is with us, ready to guide us each step of the way. When the going becomes difficult, God holds our hand or carries us over the rough and treacherous places.

Prayer: *Loving God, remind us that we don't tread the path of life alone. Help us to be ready to help our fellow travellers. Amen*

Thought for the day: Is my hand in God's, or have I strayed?

Meg Mangan (New South Wales, Australia)

Certain Hope

Read Romans 8:31–39

I am convinced that neither death nor life… nor anything else in all creation, will be able to separate us from the love of God that is in Christ Jesus our Lord.
Romans 8:38–39 (NIV)

One day, I noticed that my feet felt tingly. Within days, walking was hard. The next week, I could hardly climb the stairs at the doctor's office. The following week, I was in hospital struggling to breathe. I was diagnosed with a rare nerve disease. Nobody knew when or if I would recover. Each day I felt something new taken from me and I wondered if I would soon lose everything.

Those were overwhelming days. Hope and certainty were gone, and I was tempted to despair. But reading my Bible brought comfort. I was reminded of the hardships Paul faced. He was imprisoned, beaten, stoned, shipwrecked, hungry, cold, in danger and close to death (2 Corinthians 11:23–27). Yet Paul told us that nothing can separate us from God's love. The Bible verses did not cure me, but they helped me to keep things in perspective. They let me know that I was not alone and that the pain I felt did not mean God was angry with me or had forgotten me.

We don't know what will happen to us tomorrow or next week. Our health, our job or our home may be taken away; but even in the darkness, we can retain faith and hope if we remember that nothing can separate us from God's love.

Prayer: *O God, in the middle of life's changes, thank you for the certainty of your love. Amen*

Thought for the day: God's love will sustain us through all our tomorrows.

Loretta Goddard (South Carolina, US)

PRAYER FOCUS: THOSE SUFFERING FROM RARE ILLNESSES

Wildflowers and Weeds

Read 1 Corinthians 1:22–31

God chose what is foolish in the world to shame the wise; God chose what is weak in the world to shame the strong.
1 Corinthians 1:27 (NRSV)

My wife loves to gather wildflowers and weeds along roadsides and in abandoned fields to make bouquets. There is something about these 'lilies of the field' that brings joy and creates beauty. Unlike in a garden where beautiful flowers are a result of toil, wildflowers survive with only God's care, and they are often surprising in their beauty, abundance and fragrance.

Even the wildflowers we call weeds can have great beauty. And God apparently enjoys picking human 'weeds', each one beautiful in its own way and capable of the miraculous when combined in a bouquet pleasing to God. The genealogy of Jesus reported in Matthew 1:1–16 certainly contains people whom some would consider weeds: Rahab, a prostitute; Ruth, a Moabite foreigner; and David, an adulterer. Jesus also seemed to pick weeds as he assembled his disciples from among fishermen, tax collectors and political zealots. However, the combination of all these 'weeds' carried the message of grace and salvation throughout the world.

Prayer: *Dear Lord, thank you for using us just as we are. Help us join with others as imperfect as ourselves to work in your kingdom, as we pray, 'Father, hallowed be your name, your kingdom come. Give us each day our daily bread. Forgive us our sins, for we also forgive everyone who sins against us. And lead us not into temptation.'* * Amen*

Thought for the day: We do not have to be perfect to be used by God.

Jerry T. Lang (Michigan, US)

Greetings and Welcome!

Read Genesis 18:1–5

Abraham said to the three strangers, 'Let me get you something to eat, so you can be refreshed and then go on your way—now that you have come to your servant.'
Genesis 18:5 (NIV)

I recently moved from a relatively small community in rural West Texas to another, considerably larger, community. As a newcomer to town, I was greeted with a warm welcome by the members of the church where I was now the minister. The congregation and church staff even helped to unload the removal van. They brought dinner for my family that first night, complete with bread and dessert. Next-door neighbours popped in to introduce themselves and greeted us warmly.

The warm greeting of strangers who are now friends reminds me of the time Abraham greeted the three angelic beings. Abraham tended to his guests and offered them rest. He gave them water to wash with, prepared a meal for them, and waited attentively to serve them.

In a similar way, Christ calls us to welcome the stranger, to look after the widow and orphan, to bring comfort and welcome those whom society ignores. God challenges us to make a difference in the lives of those near us who are in need.

Prayer: *Dear Lord Jesus, help us to see your face daily in the faces of those we see who need love, help and mercy. Use us as instruments of your grace. Amen*

Thought for the day: How do I welcome the strangers near me?

Link2Life: *Seek out a new neighbour and offer a welcome.*

Jerry W. Krueger (Texas, US)

A Hope-filled Future

Read Ephesians 1:1–14

Hope does not disappoint us, because God has poured out his love into our hearts by the Holy Spirit, whom he has given us.
Romans 5:5 (NIV)

A friend told me, 'I don't hope for anything because then I'm not disappointed.' Her despairing words echoed some of her sorrow and loss, of being let down at various times throughout her life. I pray for her. I think she is probably trying to block out future pain. But I have told her that there is another way.

I've discovered God offers forgiveness and an indescribable future inheritance. I've discovered a hope that is rich, guaranteed and eternal. This isn't wishful thinking on my part; it's based on the certain promises of God. And the amazing thing is, this hope is anchored right here and now in the loving gift of the Holy Spirit, at work in all the ups and downs, the joys and sorrows that each one of us experiences. Neither my friend nor I have to fear the future because our lives are in God's hands.

Prayer: *Thank you, Lord, for the certain hope that we have in you for all we need in this life and for eternity. Amen*

Thought for the day: Our hope is anchored in God's goodness.

Link2Life: *Make a list of the signs of hope around you.*

Hilary Allen (Somerset, England)

Perfect Timing

Read Mark 6:30–44

Taking the five loaves and the two fish, [Jesus] looked up to heaven, and blessed and broke the loaves, and gave them to his disciples to set before the people.
Mark 6:41 (NRSV)

We collected food at our church one Sunday in December, and delivered it to a nursing home, a short way from our church. I was a bit worried because we seemed to have an overabundance of rice and lacked the variety of foods I thought important. The manager of the home welcomed us warmly, and we talked.

While helping us to carry in the food, the director kept repeating to a young attendant, 'We now have rice. We now have rice!'

After delivering the food, I invited the director to join us for worship. On the way to the church, I asked her why she was so insistent in telling the attendant about the rice. She said that just hours earlier they had noticed that there was no rice in the cupboards. Rice is a staple for the residents of the home, but at that moment funds were too low to purchase any.

I gave thanks to God for the multiple packages of rice that our church had donated on Sunday, and I realised that I don't have to understand what God is up to in order to be a part of it.

Prayer: *Dear Lord, grant each day an opportunity for us to share our blessings with others. May the wonder and faith of seeing the increase in the loaves and fishes remain with us always. In the name of Jesus we pray. Amen*

Thought for the day: God uses whatever we give.

Obed J. Vizcaíno N. (Zulia, Venezuela)

Grandmother God

Read Psalm 149:1–5
The Lord takes delight in his people.
Psalm 149:4 (NIV)

My grandmother was the kind of grandparent children wish for. Although we never lived close to her, she came to visit often, arriving in a cloud of lavender perfume, with cinnamon drops tucked into her pockets. As soon as she settled into the guest room, I would approach her with the big jar of buttons that my mother kept by the sewing basket. I loved to sort them into piles and to set them out in patterns as my grandmother sat beside me on the bed, patiently watching and commenting. I remember thinking how lucky I was to have a grandmother who loved buttons as much as I did. Of course, now I realise that she didn't love the buttons; she loved me.

In my memory of my grandmother is a beautiful image of God. Often, I feel God draw near, not because God is particularly interested in what I am doing but because God is interested in me and what I love. The Creator of the universe chooses to share my simple joys because this amazing God delights in me.

Prayer: *Dear God, help us to grasp the depth of your love for us. Let us sense the times that you draw near, and lead us to bring you delight. Amen*

Thought for the day: God delights in me and in each of us.

Link2Life: *Write a note to someone who has shown God to you.*

Cynthia Clarke (New York, US)

PRAYER FOCUS: GRANDPARENTS

Day by Day

Read 1 Corinthians 13:8–12

We, who with unveiled faces all reflect the Lord's glory, are being transformed into his likeness with ever-increasing glory, which comes from the Lord, who is the Spirit.
2 Corinthians 3:18 (NIV)

The other morning my six-year-old daughter brought me a book and said she wanted to read me a story. Except for one word, she read an entire children's book without stumbling or slowing down. I felt proud of her. How much she has changed over the last year! A year ago, she could read her name and one or two other words. She could write her name and count to 20. Now, as she finishes her first year of school, she is reading well and can count to over 100, and she can do simple adding and subtracting. She writes letters and reads whole books. I can see what school has done for her.

When we look at ourselves, do we similarly see what God has been doing in our lives? While the changes we undergo take time, we rest in knowing that the work God has begun in us will continue until we become like Christ (see Philippians 1:6). We see the changes when we think about our lives before we began to follow Christ and how we show our love and devotion now. In the same way as my daughter learned gradually to read, we take life one step at a time. Eventually, the little changes God is working in us will bring growth that those around us will see.

Prayer: *Dear God, help us to see how much we have grown because of abiding in you. Amen*

Thought for the day: Little by little, day by day, God is shaping me.

Link2Life: *Make a list of changes God has made in you over time.*

Zachary S. Jones (Texas, US)

Ordinary Life

Read Matthew 25:14–29

Who despises the day of small things?
Zechariah 4:10 (NIV)

First as a stay-at-home mum and later in building a career, I often felt a lack of purpose. I wanted my life to make a difference but felt that I lacked talent or specific training. One day as I read my Bible, I came to a new understanding. I saw Elisha, a hardworking farmer, ploughing with his oxen, and David, a common shepherd, tending flocks on sun-scorched plains. Zacchaeus, a tax collector, was climbing a tree, and Christ's disciples cleaned smelly fishing nets on the seashore. And there was Mary too, a young, obscure girl—the soon-to-be mother of our Lord—whom I imagined doing household chores.

Struck by the ordinariness of these people, I realised that it was not talent or training that made them champions. Their resolve to serve God faithfully in the mundane smallness of their everyday lives made them exceptional.

In the parable of the talents, the master says to two of the servants, 'You have been faithful with a few things; I will put you in charge of many things. Come and share your master's happiness!' (Matthew 25:23). Maybe we can't say we're heroes or that our lives have been noteworthy, but we can find purpose, joy and reward by living faithfully in our everyday, unspectacular routines.

Prayer: *Dear God, let us not scorn what we consider insignificant labour, but faithfully perform our everyday tasks to your glory. Amen*

Thought for the day: Any service that we dedicate to God is noble work.

Virginia Jelinek (Pennsylvania, US)

A Very Present Help

Read James 1:2–5

God is our refuge and strength, a very present help in trouble.
Psalm 46:1 (NRSV)

All my life I have been active in church, choir, pastoral work and our church's women's fellowship. When I was 20, I married the young minister who came to our church. We shared 44 years of life together and grew spiritually in our faith and commitment.

When my husband died, I worked in hospital chaplaincy training and continued serving God. However, as the years passed, I began to feel despondent about my lack of faith and trust in God. I worried and became anxious about problems I had to face alone. I prayed and searched for answers. I was greatly comforted by the words in Psalm 46:1: 'God is our refuge and strength, a very present help in trouble.'

The word 'present' is important in this verse. For me, it means that God is my constant support and friend who is with me every minute of the day and, even more importantly, every night. A sense of God's presence renewed my faith and continues to give me courage to go on and offer this assurance to others. Now I am sure we are never alone.

Prayer: *Loving God, surround those who are insecure and depressed. Help each of us to know that your love and presence are with us always. Amen*

Thought for the day: A sense of God's presence can sustain us through life's darkest nights.

Margaret Gordon (Auckland, New Zealand)

The Price Tag

Read 1 Peter 2:4–10
You were bought with a price; therefore glorify God in your body.
1 Corinthians 6:20 (NRSV)

Tom, a friend whom I admire very much, recently led our devotions in our Bible study group. He described how his church had given bicycles to a group of needy children. The bikes were brand new, still having all the shop wrappings and attached tags, but the kids were too excited to take the time to remove them. Tom said to one little boy, 'Here, let me help you take off that wrapping and price tag.'

The little boy looked up at Tom and said, 'Sir, could you leave the price on? I've never had anything with a price tag.'

That child's statement reminded me of what a blessed life I live—all because of a different kind of price tag: the cross. I take great comfort in looking at a cross, whether it is the small one in my pocket, one on the altar of my church or any other.

Unfortunately, many have hearts empty of the understanding of God's love and of the price Jesus Christ paid so we can have eternal life. When we appreciate the price Jesus paid for us, our daily lives can reflect that appreciation in ways that draw every person we encounter closer to God.

Prayer: *Dear Jesus, thank you for the price you paid for our salvation and for the many blessings we receive because of your love. Amen*

Thought for the day: Today, consider the price that Christ paid for you.

Link2Life: *Volunteer your time, your attention and your money to serve needy children in your community.*

Bill Cochran (Tennessee, US)

Too Far

Read Psalm 119:105–112

If any of you is lacking in wisdom, ask God, who gives to all generously and ungrudgingly, and it will be given you.
James 1:5 (NRSV)

'Stop!' I yelled to my four-year-old son for the third time on our walk through the neighbourhood. Once again he had gone too far from me and was dangerously close to the street. He was so distracted by the sound of the cars and the busyness of other children that he paid no attention to how far away from me he was.

I began to think of how easily we can get too far from our heavenly Father by not praying for daily guidance or not reading the Bible. Much like my son, we become distracted by what the world offers. We work longer hours in order to make more money and gain more possessions. We watch television and play computer games as entertaining distractions. These and other diversions can lead us to make wrong decisions and send us in dangerous directions, ones that are harmful to ourselves and others.

But we can be thankful that we have a Father who stays close to us. If we stray, we can call on God any time of the day or night to guide us back to the way of life that God intends—the way to joyful obedience.

Prayer: *Dear Father God, help us to stay close to you through prayer and through studying your word. Guide us to pray as if our life depends on it—because it does. Amen*

Thought for the day: In both big and small decisions, God offers us guidance.

Jerry Bragalone (Pennsylvania, US)

In God's Hands

Read Matthew 6:25–34

Everyone who asks receives, and everyone who searches finds, and for everyone who knocks, the door will be opened.
Matthew 7:8 (NRSV)

'This has nothing to do with you or your performance,' my boss said. Then she read to me a document that explained that the company was downsizing and that I would be made redundant. Suddenly, I felt demoralised and unimportant. Questions raced through my mind as I realised that I was joining the rising numbers of the unemployed. 'How can I possibly get a job at the age of 63?' I asked myself. 'Is it time to retire?' I was tempted to dwell on my loss the way I had 20 years earlier when I had lost another job.

But this time I chose to trust God. I remembered Jesus' words, 'Do not worry about your life, what you will eat or what you will drink, or about your body, what you will wear' (Matthew 6:25). I decided that worrying accomplishes nothing. Instead, I chose to take my cares to God, knowing that my Creator cares for me. Our faithful, loving God wants to give us abundant and everlasting life. My forced early retirement is in God's hands, and so far it is an adventure in faith.

Prayer: *Thank you, God, for always being with us and for showing us your love. Amen*

Thought for the day: Trusting God is a daily choice.

Sue Tornai (California, US)

Sent by God

Read Luke 7:1–10

Jesus said, 'Just as I have loved you, you also should love one another. By this everyone will know that you are my disciples, if you have love for one another.'
John 13:34–35 (NRSV)

I'm a pastor. I send out a daily email to my congregation, quoting a passage of scripture and commenting on what I see in it. One who receives these messages, like the centurion in our text, is a soldier 'under authority'. He is being deployed soon to Afghanistan. I love hearing from this man. Reflecting on what he is doing and what I see in him adds a dimension of strength to my image of the centurion.

The centurion knew Jews did not consider it permissible to enter a Gentile's home, so he was being considerate of Jesus in saying, 'I do not deserve to have you come under my roof… just say the word, and my servant will be healed.' It was amazing that this Roman had such faith in Jesus!

Back to my soldier friend. I see him and his wife and children each Wednesday night at church. Yesterday he told me again how much he appreciates the scripture emails and then said, 'My wife and girls will need some extra attention in my absence, so keep an eye on them, will you?' I, too, am 'under authority'—God's authority, as are all believers. So, for sure, this young man can count on me. It is an honour to care for God's children, and each of us is called to do it.

Prayer: *O God, help us to watch over your children near us. And help us to work for a world where war ends and soldiers never have to fight far from home. Amen*

Thought for the day: Where and to whom is God sending me today?

Dan G. Johnson (Florida, US)

Not Required

Read Matthew 25:31–46

All the nations will be gathered before [the Son of Man], and he will separate people one from another as a shepherd separates the sheep from the goats.
Matthew 25:32 (NRSV)

In our reading for today, Jesus tells us that those who care for others as if for him are the sheep who will inherit the kingdom and that the others are the goats who will not. I have had some difficulty with this passage because I'm also familiar with Ephesians 2:8–9: 'By grace you have been saved through faith, and this is not your own doing; it is the gift of God—not the result of works, so that no one may boast.' It had seemed to me that the two passages conflict with one another. Are we saved simply by accepting God's grace, as Ephesians says, or should we strive to perform good works, as Matthew says?

But then I thought about the heart of a Christian. When we accept God's grace and salvation and become believers, our heart expands—pushing us to perform good works, even though they're not technically 'required'. I see this in most Christians I know. They desire to perform these good works even though they don't see them as requirements for getting into heaven.

Christian role models help us to see that good works don't save us. Instead, good works are the natural response of Christians who are grateful for salvation and who cherish our God and our Lord Jesus Christ who sacrificed to bring salvation to us.

Prayer: *Giver of salvation, stir up in us the desire to perform good works from a grateful heart. Amen*

Thought for the day: Good works flow from a grateful heart.

Kim Sheard (Virginia, US)

Labouring in Prayer

Read Romans 15:30–32

Epaphras, who is one of you, a servant of Christ, [greets] you, always labouring fervently for you in prayers.
Colossians 4:12 (KJV)

I was approached recently by a friend who was distressed about a situation in her family, and she asked me to pray for her. I assured her I would. After uttering a quick prayer, I went about my business, never thinking of her again until I saw her a few weeks later.

Scripture tells us to pray for one another and to pray without ceasing. God hears all our prayers. But I have to admit that my prayers, unlike Epaphras', are less than an act of labour. I wonder how serious God believes we are when our manner in prayer is hurried and automatic.

Considering prayer as labour seemed strange to me until I gave it serious thought. It takes work to bring our thoughts, our hearts and our souls into deep attention to God. Our minds have a tendency to drift into the next item on our agenda, and before long, we're detached from the prayer we began.

I'd love to have an Epaphras earnestly labouring in prayer for me. And I want to be like him in the way I pray for others.

Prayer: *Dear Father, help us to be serious about our prayer life and to cherish the time we spend with you. Amen*

Thought for the day: When we commit ourselves to prayer, we open ourselves to a changed life.

Mary Baird (Texas, US)

Facing Jackals

Read Psalm 62:5–8

Those of steadfast mind you keep in peace—in peace because they trust in you.

Isaiah 26:3 (NRSV)

As I watched a documentary on lions, I saw a young cub wander away from the pride. He then found himself close to some fierce jackals. However, he did not back down; and through sheer courage in the face of danger, he managed to escape.

At times I feel like that cub, surrounded by circumstances that threaten me. Like jackals, fears lie in wait to snatch away my hope or destroy my confidence in God. But experience has shown me that if I remain in communion with God, the fears dissipate and my confidence increases.

Serving God means having faith in who God is. God is trustworthy and merciful and will not leave us in our time of need. God, our refuge and strength, will keep us in complete peace. We are not alone.

Prayer: *Dear Lord God, we give thanks that when the dangers of life assail us, you shelter us and give us strength. We pray as Jesus taught us, saying, 'Our Father which art in heaven, Hallowed be thy name. Thy kingdom come. Thy will be done, as in heaven, so in earth. Give us day by day our daily bread. And forgive us our sins; for we also forgive every one that is indebted to us. And lead us not into temptation; but deliver us from evil.' * Amen*

Thought for the day: Inner peace begins with faith in God.

Jesús Quintanilla Osorio (Quintana Roo, Mexico)

* Luke 11:2–4 (KJV)

Jesus Loves the Little Children

Read Mark 10:13–16
Jesus said to [his disciples], 'Let the little children come to me, and do not hinder them.'
Mark 10:14 (NIV)

The most horrible thing that happened in the five years I was a minister at my church was after I met Pinky. Her father had abandoned the family, including her and three sisters. Although Pinky was a bright girl, I noticed she no longer attended school regularly. A number of times I asked her why, but she didn't reply. Instead, she stopped coming to church so she wouldn't have to face my questions. To my surprise, she stopped going to school altogether and started working at a local factory with her mother and older sister. As I was wondering how I could help, I heard the horrible news that she had been brutally raped. Before I could reach out to her, she hanged herself.

If there had been someone with a heart to help her, maybe Pinky wouldn't have stopped her schooling and been put at such risk. If our church had done more to show Jesus' love, perhaps she would be alive today. I am deeply sad about Pinky, but I thank God for her too. She changed my life and my ministry. I have started a home where at-risk girls can find shelter and help. As God allows, I want to offer them hope and a future.

I want to have a heart like Jesus.

Prayer: *O Lord, give us hearts like yours to love and care for the young people in our life. Show us what to do. Amen*

Thought for the day: When we show Christ's love to a child, we change the future.

S. Rajan (Kerala, India)

'Get a Grip'

Read Acts 9:26–31

Let us… no longer pass judgment on one another, but resolve instead never to put a stumbling block or hindrance in the way of another.
Romans 14:13 (NRSV)

At a local fast-food restaurant, my wife and I heard the screams of an unhappy toddler. Something had displeased him, and he was—repeatedly—making his mother aware of this displeasure. She finally picked him up, held him at eye level and said firmly, 'Get a grip, Justin!' Those words have become an inside joke when either of us becomes upset or complains excessively and repeatedly about some minor issue.

The incident reminded us of our own impatience with our children when we were young parents. But beyond that, on a spiritual level, it exemplifies too often the unspoken (and sometimes spoken) demand from some seasoned saints to less mature believers. I have come to understand that both spiritual and physical babies behave like babies.

In my early Christian experience, some believers were rigid about rules and lists of acceptable behaviour. The unspoken attitude was 'get a grip'. But a handful of believers encouraged me when I felt discouraged or failed God. Thank God for those unpretentious saints in my life who, like Barnabas, were a source of consolation. I want to pass on that light and consolation that others shared with me.

Prayer: *Dear Lord, help me to encourage someone today. Amen*

Thought for the day: Do I encourage or discourage others?

Link2Life: *Be a Barnabas to some new Christian floundering to find sure footing in their new faith.*

Thomas Buice (Florida, US)

PRAYER FOCUS: THOSE YOUNG IN THE FAITH

Sowing Tears

Read Psalm 126

May those who sow in tears reap with shouts of joy. Those who go out weeping, bearing the seed for sowing, shall come home with shouts of joy, carrying their sheaves.
Psalm 126:5–6 (NRSV)

This year my youngest daughter received for her birthday a kit with all she needed to grow flowers. On a sunny day in June we filled the pot with soil, planted the seeds according to the instructions, and set it on our patio. Over the coming weeks we faithfully watered the plants, anticipating a colourful display of flowers. Slowly, we saw the transition from seed to seedling to bud to flower. It's hard to fathom how such a rich tapestry of colour could come from such an unspectacular beginning. Seeds that are no more than grey flecks are the genesis of a rainbow of colour—green, blue, red, orange and yellow.

The flowers reminded me of the words of Psalm 126—that our sorrows can be the seeds of joy, an un-wonderful beginning that brings a wonderful crop. The psalmist sings of God's redemption in bringing back captives and restoring their fortunes, taking them out of their captivity and deprivation. In sadness can be seeds that God will cultivate to grow a rainbow of joy.

Prayer: *Dear God of all comfort, help us to rest in the hope that you will bring joy out of our sorrow. Amen*

Thought for the day: God can transform sorrow to joy.

Philip Huber (New York, US)

'No, Lord!'

Read Acts 11:1–9

Moses said, 'No, Lord, don't send me.'
Exodus 4:10 (GNB)

In worship last Sunday morning, we sang a hymn asking Jesus to be the Lord of our lives. As I joined in, I sincerely meant those words. Later, on the way home from an afternoon drive, we passed an elderly neighbour, recently widowed, who was walking slowly up a long hill. My husband stopped to offer her a lift home and, as she climbed into the car, I inwardly sensed God saying to me, 'Invite her to your house for tea.' My immediate, inward response was, 'No, Lord' because I was looking forward to a long, quiet reading time with my feet up. Sunday is, after all, a day of rest.

We took our lonely friend to her house and came home. But some words I had recently read in the book of Acts kept playing through my mind. When given a clear-cut instruction from God, the apostle Peter had protested, 'No, Lord!' without realising what a contradiction that protest was. 'No' and 'Lord' don't fit together.

I have decided to turn my no to a yes by inviting my neighbour out for a stroll next Sunday, with tea to follow. I do hope she'll come.

Prayer: *Dear Lord, help us to answer with a willing yes when you have instructions for us, showing our love for you in quick and glad obedience. Amen*

Thought for the day: Saying yes to God opens the door to opportunities we wouldn't want to miss.

Link2Life: *Invite someone who lives alone to share a meal.*

Elaine Brown (Perthshire, Scotland)

Beauty for Ashes

Read Isaiah 61:1–3

God… has sent me to bring good news to the oppressed.
Isaiah 61:1 (NRSV)

After an exhausting afternoon of teaching, when I had lost control of both my students and my temper, I began the walk home. I was surrounded by ugliness. The streets of the city were strewn with litter and smelled of sewage. The inner-city children I work with struggle with many problems, and I was failing to gain self-control and good stewardship of my mind, body and finances. 'Where,' I wondered, 'is the hope for this city, for these children and for me?'

Taking a shortcut, I followed abandoned railway tracks, carefully placing my foot with each step to avoid shards of glass strewn along the rails. Then I looked ahead. With my focus off the ugly details that surrounded me, I saw something beautiful. The light of the setting sun hit each of those broken, dirty shards of glass; the shards reflected a dazzling brilliance. Rubbish became something altogether stunning when bathed in the light of the afternoon sun.

I realised that there is hope for this city, for these children and even for me as the light of Christ transforms the broken and useless into the useful and whole. God gives 'beauty for ashes'. I realised that I do not have to allow the unpleasant details of life to eclipse the brilliance of God's love!

Prayer: *Dear God, give us a glimpse of you in the difficult circumstances of daily life. Let us see and reflect your transforming light. Amen*

Thought for the day: God's light transforms us.

Link2Life: *Volunteer to work with an after-school club or with a disadvantaged student who struggles to develop basic skills.*

Aaron McNutt (North Carolina, US)

Forgiven For Ever

Read Psalm 103:1–18

The Lord says, 'I will put my laws in their hearts, and I will write them on their minds… Their sins and lawless acts I will remember no more.'
Hebrews 10:16–17 (NIV)

My wife and I lived in a flat for a few years. There was a flat above us and one beneath us. The floors were thin, and we heard every footstep and movement of our upstairs neighbours. We sympathised with the family living below us and made every effort to tiptoe and be cautious out of courtesy to them. Tiptoeing and speaking in soft tones became our lifestyle. We did our best to catch anything we dropped before it hit the floor. When something did hit the floor, we would look down at the floor and say apologetically, 'Sorry, guys!'

Eventually we moved into a house. However, for months we continued to tiptoe and apologise to the floor when we dropped something. Then we would realise we were not in the flat anymore. Though people no longer lived below us, we behaved as if they did.

That is often how we live in regard to our sin. The Bible says Christ is faithful to forgive us our sins and cleanse us from all unrighteousness. Unfortunately, even after we are forgiven, we sometimes live as if forgiveness never occurred. That is just as silly as living as if we have neighbours below us when we do not. God is trustworthy, and when we ask for forgiveness, God gives it.

Prayer: *Dear Father, thank you for forgiving and cleansing us of sin. Help us not to feel burdened by forgiven sin. Amen*

Thought for the day: When God forgives our sin, it is gone for ever.

Frankie J. Melton, Jr (South Carolina, US)

PRAYER FOCUS: THOSE LIVING AS IF THEY ARE NOT FORGIVEN

God's Children?

Read Luke 10:25–37

Love your enemies and pray for those who persecute you, so that you may be children of your Father in heaven.
Matthew 5:44–45 (NRSV)

A heated discussion was going on in the church car park. I wanted to leave, so I tried to slip past my friends.

'Come here!' they called. 'Answer a question.'

'Who are God's children?' one asked, continuing, 'All are God's children and made in his image. Some get lost and decide not to follow God, but he still loves them.'

The other said, 'We are not all God's children. Unbelieving, sinful people can't be God's children. My mother has brought hurt to everyone her life ever touched. She isn't a child of God.'

I stood there unsure what to say. 'Help me, Lord!' I prayed. Suddenly I knew what to say. 'I guess it's not important.'

'Not important?' they asked in surprise.

'I can't know who all the children of God are, but I know I am to treat each person I meet as one of God's beloved children. Jesus said to love even our enemies and to pray for those who hurt us.'

My friend with the hurtful mother started to cry. Then we prayed together.

Prayer: *Heavenly Father, help us treat everyone as your children, even those who hurt us. Then everyone will know we belong to you. Amen*

Thought for the day: Our loving ways can make people want to know God better.

Susan Boltz (Ohio, US)

The Clock is Ticking

Read Proverbs 3:1–8

I trust in you, O Lord… My times are in your hands.
Psalm 31:14–15 (NIV)

I seem to spend a great deal of my day fighting against the clock. There are always more things to be done than hours in the day to do them. Sleeping, nurturing my marriage and taking time with each of my children can't be done quickly. And it seems that before I've blinked, another day has gone. Often the tasks don't seem worth the time they consume. Little time seems to be left to do the things I really want to do.

I never expected life to look like this. As a teenager and young adult, I prayed that I wouldn't be average. I wanted to be different and to change the world. I didn't expect life to involve rushing around washing socks.

How relieved I am, therefore, to discover that God can and does make the ordinary extraordinary. Day by day, as I follow God's paths—as I trust and obey—I become more content. I've seen that however mundane tasks may seem, small acts can have greater impact than anyone could have imagined. Who knows, for instance, how my children might change the world for God? What I do know is that God goes ahead of me and walks beside me. God is not restricted or pressured by clocks or calendars, and my times are in God's hands.

Prayer: *Dear Father God, help us to know your peace as we walk through the days you have ordained for us. Amen*

Thought for the day: When we obey in trust, God can use our small actions to accomplish much.

Jenny Sanders (Hampshire, England)

PRAYER FOCUS: THOSE WHO FEEL HARASSED

Spiritual Gifts

Read 1 Corinthians 12:4–11

To each is given the manifestation of the Spirit for the common good.
1 Corinthians 12:7 (NRSV)

Once while teaching a Sunday school class, I asked the children if they knew who enjoyed the fruit of the fruit tree—the tree itself, or the one who planted it. The children knew that the tree produces good fruit not for its own enjoyment but for others. If we apply this analogy to ourselves, we see that our gifts from God are not meant simply for our own enjoyment either. God's word says that our gifts are for the benefit of all; they are 'for the common good'.

The gifts we have indeed come from God, given to us so that we can use them for others. Unfortunately, we sometimes lose sight of this truth when we use our gifts to promote ourselves. Sometimes we use them to chase after riches, recognition or other self-centred ambitions. Then, like a tool in the hands of the wrong master, our gifts are not used for God's purposes.

When we use our gifts apart from God's intent, whatever we achieve will amount to nothing. But when we use them for God's glory, we become a part of the work that the Spirit is doing.

Prayer: *Dear Lord Jesus Christ, thank you for the gifts you have given us. Help us see how we can use our gifts to build up your church. Amen*

Thought for the day: What gifts do you have, and how can you use them to benefit others?

Link2Life: *Carry out a spiritual-gifts inventory.*

Sum Wei Siang (Perak, Malaysia)

Many Gifts, One Spirit

Read Acts 2:1–13

Beloved, since God loved us so much, we also ought to love one another.
1 John 4:11 (NRSV)

During our first Christmas season at Africa University in Zimbabwe, we missed the seasonal changes that herald Christmas at home; even more, we missed our family. It dawned on me that we were not alone in yearning for familiar faces and the warmth of familial love. At least ten different nations were represented in the university student body that year, and virtually none of the students from other countries could go home for the holidays.

Then the Spirit gave me an idea: invite all the students staying on campus to our home for a Christmas Eve dinner. We invited each to bring a dish from their native land. What a feast, and what an amazing celebration we experienced! After dinner, one by one, the students shared a favourite Christmas tradition and taught us, in their various languages, a song that celebrated Jesus' birth. We sang in many tongues, but we were one in the Spirit. That year, we celebrated Pentecost at Christmas.

It must have been similar for those from many nations crowded into Jerusalem at the first Pentecost. The wind of the Spirit whirled around them, filling them with awe as they heard the story of Jesus' life, his crucifixion and his resurrection. Believers discovered a new family in Christ—and the Spirit still calls each of us to help build that community of love.

Prayer: *Spirit of God, fill each of us afresh. In every person we encounter may we find our brother or our sister. Amen*

Thought for the day: Believers in Christ are one family living in many places.

Paul W. Chilcote (Ohio, US)

Stay Awake!

Read Luke 12:35–44
Keep awake… for you know neither the day nor the hour.
Matthew 25:13 (NRSV)

The first day of the work week had not got off to a good start. First I had to go back home to collect a bag that I had forgotten. Then I left the bag behind on the luggage rack in the train. I had to go back for it again, and this time I had to explain to the ticket inspector and the driver what had happened. I know I am not the only one to whom these kinds of things happen, especially after a long weekend. Often we sleep on the go, automatically move in the necessary direction and float along the usual river of our life.

Our relationship with God can become like this as well. We go to church on Sundays purely out of habit. We neither change nor grow spiritually. We are happy with the way things are. We put off reading the Bible until later, or talking about our faith to a non-believer until next week or next month, or taking on a new way of ministry until next year. It is as if we have become frozen in our faith. But God calls us to be always ready for Christ's coming.

God calls us to pray without ceasing and to act and live each day as if it were our last. We cannot answer that call casually or haphazardly. A life of true faith requires committed, intentional walking with Jesus Christ and following in his footsteps.

Prayer: *Dear Lord, help us to keep awake and to make sure that we always have enough oil in our lamps to be ready to meet you. Amen*

Thought for the day: What am I doing today for God, for the church, for other people?

Zhanna Kim (Moscow, Russia)

God's Complete Love

Read Matthew 10:29–31

Even the very hairs of your head are all numbered.
Matthew 10:30 (NIV)

Soon after my daughter, Gracie, turned three, she started chemo-
therapy. Six months of treatment were needed to help her fight a
rare form of eye cancer. As I contemplated what lay ahead, I was
paralysed by fear. 'How could this be happening?' I asked myself.
'Why my daughter?' I asked God.

Shortly after her first treatment, Gracie's hair began to fall out.
My heart broke when she handed me a fistful of long blonde curls.
'Help me comfort her,' I quietly asked God. 'I can't do this without
you.'

Immediately, an amazing calm came over me. I remembered
Matthew 10:30. God's love for Gracie is so complete that 'even the
very hairs of [her] head are all numbered'. I held Gracie and lovingly
brushed her hair. As more of her hair fell out, I reassured her that
God knows everything that is happening to us. No matter what we
are going through, God is with us, holding us as I held her.

Now, years later, when I brush Gracie's long, blonde hair I am
reminded of God's love. When I look through scripture, I read that
God can be trusted. Jesus says that God is aware of everything
that happens even to the sparrows. No matter what we are going
through, whether illness, loneliness or separation, God is with us.
God values us enough to count each strand of our hair.

Prayer: *Thank you, God, for holding us when times are tough. Amen*

Thought for the day: God values us down to each hair on our head.

Link2Life: *Sit quietly and picture yourself being held tenderly by God.*

Angela Pisel (North Carolina, US)

PRAYER FOCUS: CHILDREN BEING TREATED FOR CANCER

Choosing the Best

Read Luke 10:38–42

Seek first [God's] kingdom and his righteousness, and all these things will be given to you as well.
Matthew 6:33 (NIV)

Recently, while weeding my garden, I saw half a dozen sturdy yellow sprouts that didn't look like any of the vegetables I had planted. I soon realised that they were pumpkin plants, growing from seeds that had been in the compost I added to the soil. At first I was excited; pumpkins are delicious! I quickly remembered, though, that pumpkins are plants that could easily take over my small garden, leaving no room for anything else. Every day since then, I've found more pumpkin seedlings—sometimes as many as 30 in one day! I'm allowing one plant to grow, but the others I diligently remove.

Like my garden, I have limited space; I also have limited time. If I'm not careful, even good things—like the pumpkin plants in my garden—can easily take too much of my life, leaving no room for better things. Work is good, but it's not always the best choice. Tending relationships with friends is good, but spending time with friends is not always the best use of time. To have a balanced life, I need to check my heart as I check my garden to make sure that good activities are not crowding out the best in my life.

Prayer: *Dear God, help us to cultivate our hearts and lives wisely, giving space and time to what is most important. Teach us to seek your kingdom and righteousness above all else. Amen*

Thought for the day: What is good can crowd out what is best.

Link2Life: *Chart how you've spent your time in the last week. What priorities does your chart reveal?*

Amy Peterson (Arkansas, US)

Teenage Saints

Read Micah 4:1–3; 6:6–8
Let justice roll down like waters, and righteousness like an ever-flowing stream.
Amos 5:24 (NRSV)

In my country, South Africa, 16 June is a public holiday called Youth Day. On this day more than 30 years ago, young people of Soweto, a black township, peacefully demonstrated against our oppressive, apartheid government. Many lost their lives—some as young as 14 years old—when the demonstrators were attacked. Many predicted a gloomy end for us. Most found it difficult to imagine a future of peace and hope—gifts that our loving God earnestly desires for all humanity.

As the world gathered in South Africa for the football World Cup competition a year ago, many thousands came here to support their national teams. Once the world's pariah because of apartheid, South Africa had become the world's host. The bravery shown by those young people decades ago has led to my country's transformation. This shows that with God's help and the actions of brave people, anything is possible.

History moves me to give thanks to God for brave people who, through the ages, have stood against injustice. Our world will always need Christians to continue to say to the darkness, 'I beg to differ.' No amount of darkness can put out God's light. As Romans 8:28 tells us, out of bad God brings good.

Prayer: *O God, give us brave hearts and the will to make this world more like you want it to be. Amen*

Thought for the day: God's eternal desire for justice can be embodied in our lives.

Roland Rink (Gauteng, South Africa)

The Anchor Holds

Read Hebrews 6:10–19

We have this hope, a sure and steadfast anchor of the soul.
Hebrews 6:19 (NRSV)

I huddled in a corner, tears flowing. Though the marks on my body were new, they were not unfamiliar. For years I had prayed for my husband, a Christian, and for an end to the beatings he inflicted in his rages. God had been my anchor as I grew up, and I wondered why he had not intervened to stop the abuse.

Earlier that evening as I left to attend a Christian concert, my husband had told me not to come back. When I returned, he threw me into a wall. This time, to my amazement, through my tears the words 'I want a divorce' fell out of my mouth. And as they did, I felt the chains of fear and oppression lift. God whispered to me that I would never be hurt again by this man. That night, my Anchor held.

Until that very moment, I never understood how much God loved me or the vastness of God's grace. God does not intend for any of us to be oppressed and abused, and God wanted a safe harbour for me. I am a living example of the words from the song, 'the anchor holds, though the ship is battered'. I was battered, and I thank God for being my steadfast and true anchor. God helped me to leave the raging sea of abuse and led me to the freedom Christ offers and wants for each of us.

Prayer: *O God, free us from all that oppresses us. Amen*

Thought for the day: God calls us from bondage to freedom and fullness of life.

Tricia S. (Tennessee, US)

Come Home!

Read Luke 15:4–10
Pray continually.
1 Thessalonians 5:17 (NIV)

In a meditation I wrote some years ago for *The Upper Room*, I described the parallel between training young pea plants to grow correctly on a trellis and training our children in the ways of the Lord. A new aspect of this annual practice recently occurred to me during a time of despair over our adult children.

Some of our more mature pea plants had been firmly attached to the base of the trellis, but as they grew, their stems went off in all directions and the tendrils could not reach the trellis. These plants were windblown, fallen and in danger of snapping at their stems. So I have had carefully to bend the plants and use supporting string to keep the plants upright, so that they can again attach to the trellis and be able to set pods. This reminded me that no matter how far we may stray from the Lord, God always reaches out to offer support and love, guiding us back.

I have shared something of the agony of the father of the prodigal son (see Luke 15), and indeed, of God's heart, since our beloved children are distant from the Lord. Scripture encourages us to 'pray continually'. This is a large part of keeping a faithful lookout for the spiritual return of those prodigals in our biological or spiritual families. We long to welcome them back with immeasurable love, just as God welcomes every one of us.

Prayer: *Dear God of prodigals, thank you for the assurance of your limitless love for every sheep who returns to you. In Jesus' name. Amen*

Thought for the day: God never gives up on anyone.

Ann Sloane (New South Wales, Australia)

My Abba

Read Romans 8:12–17

God sent his Son… so that we might receive adoption as children. And because you are children, God has sent the Spirit of his Son into our hearts, crying, 'Abba! Father!'
Galatians 4:4–6 (NRSV)

My father died in 1979 from cancer. He had served as a police officer with the government of Karnataka in South India. We called him 'Appa', which means 'father' in Kannada, our local language. As was the custom during that time, daughters could not have open relationships or conversations with their fathers. Though we respected and honoured our parents, we expressed our love to them only by obedience, never in words.

Only after his death did I realise how much I missed him. I longed to hold him and express the love and gratitude I could not express when he was living. Every day I think about him and thank God for giving him to me to be my father.

Whenever I read Romans 8:15, I rejoice in the everlasting love and concern of God and reflect on the kindness and mercy God shows in taking away our fear and calling us 'children of God'.

We can also show our gratitude for this amazing love by reaching out to others to share the love of God with them.

Prayer: *O God, we thank you for calling us your children. Help us to love you as you have loved us. Amen*

Thought for the day: All of us have a loving 'Abba' in heaven.

Mary Joyce (Karnataka, India)

PRAYER FOCUS: SOMEONE WHO LONGS TO KNOW A FATHER'S LOVE

Lavish Love

Read 1 John 4:7–18

How great is the love the Father has lavished on us, that we should be called children of God!
1 John 3:1 (NIV)

I've forgotten his name, but I will never forget his words. I met him while on a college-choir tour. As he drove my friend and me to his house for the night, he told us about his family. After affectionately describing his wife and younger daughter, he talked about his elder daughter—an eight-year-old girl. The father's eyes gleamed as he raved about his love for this daughter. What he said next surprised us: 'She has Down's Syndrome. She will never read or write or do many things that other children do.' He paused thoughtfully and then continued, 'Yet the way I love her has helped me to understand God's love for me.'

I desperately needed those words then and, I confess, I still need them now. I think I am hard-headed. I often forget that God's love for us has nothing to do with our performance. We can do nothing to make God love us any more than he does; we can do nothing that will make God love us any less. God loves us and delights in us simply because he is our Father.

Prayer: *Heavenly Father, help us to live each day in the light of your love. Amen*

Thought for the day: God's love for us has nothing to do with our accomplishments.

Ben Styles (Tennessee, US)

Tidal Reminder

Read Lamentations 3:22–24

Jesus Christ is the same yesterday and today and forever.
Hebrews 13:8 (NIV)

The back porch of a log cabin we rent for holidays looks across a tidal creek lined by colourful houses and boats of all shapes and sizes. Each morning we wake to a new view, according to the state of the tide. Sometimes the water laps at the bright sea-grass islands and reflects the jetties and vividly painted mooring buoys. At other times the water recedes, leaving boats stranded at odd angles on the shell-spattered mud. The reflections are confined to a ribbon of water snaking down the middle of the creek.

I live in a town far from the sea. But on holiday, I am reminded of the constant change of tides, flowing in and out twice a day, altering the scenery hour by hour, varying according to the changes of the tides. Behind the changes, the moon drives the steady rhythm, reliable and unstoppable. Each day is the same, yet each day is different.

This truth causes me to think of God. How wonderful that the God we worship is unchanging, 'yesterday and today and forever'! God's love is reliable and unstoppable. Yet it is also 'new every morning' (Lamentations 3:23). Each time we open our eyes to a new day, the possibilities God offers us are endless and always fresh.

Prayer: *Creator of goodness and beauty, in each new day, encourage us by your faithfulness and delight us by the constant surprises you bring. Amen*

Thought for the day: God has surprises in store for us every day.

Liz Howden (Cheshire, England)

Give and Let Live

Read Luke 6:27–36

Jesus said, 'Give to everyone who begs from you.'
Luke 6:30 (NRSV)

A colleague and I were discussing how to respond to those who ask for a handout. I've had similar conversations with various people, and I have come to this peaceful decision: to give to anyone who asks of me. I may or may not have exactly what they are looking for—whether it is a homeless person asking for change or someone who claims to have a broken-down car at a petrol station. But I take comfort in knowing that I am following Jesus' command, 'Give to everyone who begs from you.' I have decided to give without questioning whether there is a real need or not.

I believe Jesus calls us to respond with compassion. What recipients do with our donations is between them and God. I hope they may be inspired to pass the kindness on. Or, because someone answered their cry for help, maybe they will know they are not invisible. In any case, I pray my gift makes their day a little brighter. My thank-you is usually a smile and a 'God bless you.'

I find great satisfaction knowing that I have answered Christ's call, even though I know I have been taken advantage of more than once. I am fortunate to have more than I need and to have the means to share with those who ask.

Prayer: *Please make us more aware, dear Lord, of daily reminders of your call to give—even when the calls come from never-dreamed-of people and places. Amen*

Thought for the day: True gifts come with no strings attached.

Nanci H. Lamar (Tennessee, US)

Family Resemblance

Read 1 Peter 1:13–16

Be imitators of me, as I am of Christ.
1 Corinthians 11:1 (NRSV)

My six-year-old daughter, Jessica, came home from school smiling. She hugged me and said gleefully, 'Daddy, Daddy, I met a man today who asked me whether I'm your daughter. When I said, "Yes" he smiled and said that I look like you.'

'Is that the reason you are happy?' I asked her.

'Yes,' she replied, 'I'm always happy when people tell me that I look like you.' I was happy when my daughter expressed joy because she resembles me.

Jessica's behaviour reminded me of what God wants for us. I realised that as a child of God, I am meant to resemble my maker and to show God's attributes so that others will see them. So are we all. If we do that, others will be drawn to God's family because of seeing Christ in us.

Prayer: *Dear God, help us to exhibit your divine attributes so that others will see and glorify you. As Jesus taught us, we pray, 'Our Father which art in heaven, Hallowed be thy name. Thy kingdom come. Thy will be done in earth, as it is in heaven. Give us this day our daily bread. And forgive us our debts, as we forgive our debtors. And lead us not into temptation, but deliver us from evil: For thine is the kingdom, and the power, and the glory, for ever. Amen.'* *

Thought for the day: As we strive to reflect God's nature, others will see God's love in us.

Francis Sackitey (Eastern Region, Ghana)

PRAYER FOCUS: CHILDREN OF ABSENT FATHERS
* Matthew 6:9–13 (KJV)

A Ram in the Thicket

Read Genesis 22:1–14

The Lord says, 'I give water in the wilderness, rivers in the desert, to give drink to my chosen people, the people whom I formed for myself so that they might declare my praise.'
Isaiah 43:20–21 (NRSV)

For the past year or more, economic conditions worldwide have been difficult. Most of us have family, friends and colleagues who have suffered pay cuts or the loss of jobs, and perhaps are living under the threat of further layoffs ourselves. It seems that nobody is exempt from this crisis. Some of us get up every day questioning, 'Is this the day?' We rehearse reasons why our job is more important than our fellow workers' when in fact we know that each of our jobs is vital and each of us is equally important.

As I have become more and more dispirited, I remember the biblical account of Abraham preparing to take his son Isaac up on the mountain and sacrifice him. As a result of Abraham's trust and commitment, God provided a way out for him by sending a ram to sacrifice instead of Isaac.

Companies and organisations are doing all they can to survive. I firmly believe that no matter how difficult life seems, even in the throes of such a bad economy, we can trust God. We can stay committed to doing that, knowing that we are important to God and believing that God will provide 'a ram in the thicket' for us.

Prayer: *Faithful God, no matter how difficult our circumstances may get, help us to focus on who we are and to whom we belong, trusting that you alone will supply all that we need. Amen*

Thought for the day: God, not a job or our bank account, is the source of our security.

Shawana A. Brown (Tennessee, US)

Confession is Necessary

Read Galatians 2:15–20

If anyone does sin, we have an advocate with the Father, Jesus Christ the righteous; and he is the atoning sacrifice for our sins.
1 John 2:1–2 (NRSV)

The air conditioning unit in our home needs maintenance every three months to clear the accumulation of dust from the air filter. Otherwise the air duct gets blocked and water from condensation starts to drip inside our house.

Similarly, wrongs that accumulate in a Christian's life can be a hindrance. However, God has provided a way to clear this accumulation of sin from our lives. 1 John 1:9 reminds us, 'If we confess our sins, he who is faithful and just will forgive us our sins and cleanse us from all unrighteousness.'

When we try to live the Christian life in our own strength only, we will struggle and feel defeated. But we can experience victorious life in Christ when we confess our sins and depend on the power of the Holy Spirit.

Prayer: *Gracious Father, thank you that we can confess our sins, for you are faithful to forgive us. Amen*

Thought for the day: Confession is necessary to live a victorious life in Christ.

Mary Ng Shwu Ling (Singapore)

Missed Opportunities

Read 2 Corinthians 8:8–15

Whoever has two coats much share with anyone who has none; and whoever has food must do likewise.
Luke 3:11 (NRSV)

Recently I sorted through my parents' belongings. In the attic I found duplicate sets of household items—kitchen utensils, furniture, electronics and linen. These items had been stored through many hot summers and cold winters, rendering most unusable. Accumulated over the years when family members passed away, they had been stored as keepsakes. They also reflected a need to save for a 'rainy day', born of my father's being brought up in poverty before and during the Great Depression years. These items would have been eagerly received by less fortunate people had they been offered. Certainly, my parents intended no harm by storing the excess items. Nonetheless, they missed opportunities to enrich the lives of others.

I learned from my attic experience to focus on God's expectation that we attend to the needy, those without the basics of life, and to be satisfied with fewer material possessions. We love our brothers and sisters by looking to their interests, not to only our own.

Prayer: *Dear God, help us to be realistic about our needs and to remember that meeting the needs of others is our responsibility also. Amen*

Thought for the day: What excess possessions can I give to help others?

Link2Life: *Go through your house, identify 'extra' items that could help others, and donate them.*

John H. McKnight (North Carolina, US)

PRAYER FOCUS: THOSE WHO HAVE 'LOST EVERYTHING'

God's Signal

Read 1 Samuel 24:1–10

Wait for the Lord; be strong, and let your heart take courage; wait for the Lord!
Psalm 27:14 (NRSV)

We were going through tough times; problems seemed to surface everywhere. Taking a Christian stand daily at work was difficult. Threatening telephone calls became a routine; and then our car was set on fire. Our family and friends suggested that we ask for a transfer to a safer place because our lives were at risk. However, we were aware that God had led us to this difficult place. We placed the matter before God, seeking direction.

In today's reading, we see that David had a good opportunity to kill King Saul. But David did not kill the king because he knew that Saul was God's anointed one, and David hoped that God would bring an end to the misery he experienced at Saul's hands. David did not do anything to move toward becoming king. Instead, he waited patiently for God to act.

David became our model. As time passed, the threatening calls became fewer and finally stopped altogether. The thought of moving also slowly dimmed. The situation improved slowly, and after two years we were transferred to another hospital far away. We knew the transfer was God's signal for us to move on, and we did so. We were filled with praise for God because our new setting was beautiful and the change proved good for us both physically and spiritually.

Prayer: *Dear Lord, thank you for your wonderful love. In times of persecution, help us to trust you for strength and courage. Amen*

Thought for the day: When we know we're obeying God, we can endure whatever comes at us.

Pramila Barkataki (Maharashtra, India)

Enduring Love

Read Luke 15:11–32
Love never fails.
1 Corinthians 13:8 (NIV)

My mum and dad were hard workers and took delight in sending my sister and me to college. But I wasted the opportunity. I did not want my parents to know, but the day came when the truth was made known to them.

They reminded me of the Bible story about the prodigal son and his loving father. Luke 15:20 says that the prodigal's father 'ran to his son, threw his arms around him and kissed him'. What makes this verse so amazing is that the father gave this unfailing love to the son who had earlier said to him, 'Give me my share of the estate' (Luke 15:12)—essentially 'I wish you were dead.' Daily the father watched for this son's return, and then he acted with unfailing love.

Unfailing love always looks for reconciliation. Enduring love quickly offers forgiveness and mercy, which lead to unity and wholeness. The father's enduring love resulted in restoration for the returning prodigal. The father said, 'Put a ring on his finger and sandals on his feet' (Luke 15:22), reinstating his son to a place of honour in the family.

My parents' love and support never failed as I reorganised my life. This is the love God has for each of us, every day.

Prayer: *Thank you, God, for your enduring, unfailing love. Help us to be instruments of restoration for those who have wandered from you. Amen*

Thought for the day: We serve the God of forgiveness and mercy.

Michael D. Smith (South Carolina, US)

PRAYER FOCUS: PRODIGALS

An Adventure in Prayer

Read John 10:1–10

Jesus said, 'I came that they may have life, and have it abundantly.'
John 10:10 (NRSV)

I kissed my young son goodbye and prayed for him as he went for emergency surgery. However, my prayer seemed to bounce back like an echo. I was consumed with fear.

I sat in an easy chair in the waiting room. Glancing over the magazines, I picked up a small green booklet with an intriguing title: *Adventures in Prayer*. Since my prayers felt lifeless, I knew I needed help. The words from author Catherine Marshall were exciting because she prayed about her everyday needs. Her relationship with God sounded personal. What did all of this mean? I had prayed for years in church. But something was missing. I began to see that my faith was based more on dutiful religion than on a growing relationship with God.

At that moment I prayed the first exciting prayer I had ever uttered. 'Lord, I don't know you. Please help me.' The peace and joy that came to my heart was a new experience. It helped me to understand that God had heard me.

My son's surgery was a success, but the spiritual surgery of my soul had just begun. Since I learned to see God as my friend, life has never been the same.

Prayer: *Friend and Redeemer, thank you for those who write words of hope that lead us closer to your abundant life. Amen*

Thought for the day: Knowing God is the key to powerful and fulfilling prayer.

Lucy Neeley Adams (North Carolina, US)

Does Practice Make Perfect?

Read Colossians 1:18–29

God proves his love for us in that while we still were sinners Christ died for us.
Romans 5:8 (NRSV)

Mrs Youngholm came to our house once a week for my piano lesson. After checking my posture and hand position, she would have me play. If she was satisfied with my progress, she'd put a gold star at the top of the page in my music book. Her parting words were always, 'Practice makes perfect.'

Sometimes when I practised on my own, I'd get sloppy and careless. But Mum would notice and make me go back over the music until I got it right. Then she would remind me again, 'Practice makes perfect.'

Did I become an accomplished musician? No. In my case, practice didn't make perfect. However, I retain a love of music and good habits that are helpful in other areas of my life, and I don't regret having had the training.

Now, as a Christian, I practise spiritual disciplines, but they don't make me perfect either. That's because what I do myself can't make me perfect. Only what Jesus did on the cross can. Jesus took the penalty for my sins on himself so I could be reconciled to God. Because of Christ, we don't have to be perfect. Now my music is all about thanking and praising God. It's not perfect, but to God it's a joyful sound.

Prayer: *Dear Lord, please help us always to find new ways to praise you. In Jesus' name we pray. Amen*

Thought for the day: God doesn't expect us to be perfect.

Ellen Cardwell (California, US)

PRAYER FOCUS: MUSIC TEACHERS AND STUDENTS

The Look of Love

Leaving a community worship service, I found myself walking beside a friend from another church whom I hadn't seen in several months. After we greeted one another, she said, 'You look great! Something's different—you're just glowing!' She looked intently into my eyes and then said, 'I know what it is! You're in love, aren't you? That's it!' She was right; I had fallen in love after years of being alone. I know someone else who says he can see an unusual radiance in those who have a close relationship with God.

Apparently I am not as sensitive as either of these two people. I can't tell this much about others simply by looking at them. I do believe, however, that encountering and feeling love transforms us. In fact, scripture says so (see 2 Corinthians 3:16–18, NRSV).

Most of us have noticed people whose faces show suffering and tension, and so we can understand how being freed from concern could change someone's appearance. Paul wrote that knowing Christ frees us and transforms us not just superficially but fundamentally (see Romans 12:1–18 and 2 Corinthians 5:17). But how does transformation come about?

Transformation is not magic, and it is not instantaneous. It happens gradually as we spend time with other believers. In another place Paul urged, 'Be imitators of me, as I am of Christ' (1 Corinthians 11:1). Many of us would probably hesitate to say that. But we all also know people who by their example make us want to be more steadfast, more loving, more gentle, more forgiving—in other words, more like Christ. The transformation that occurs in Christian community is not born of white-knuckle obedience or in response to criticism and pressure to conform. What lastingly transforms us and others is what that friend somehow saw in my face that day: love.

Jesus said, 'Where two or three are gathered in my name, I am there among them' (Matthew 18:20). Christ is present in our interaction with other believers. As we worship, study, pray and serve alongside them, as we come to know our brothers and sisters more deeply and allow ourselves to be known by them, we grow also to know Christ better because each of us shows a part of Christ to the rest of us. We help one another 'as iron sharpens iron' (Proverbs 27:17) to reflect Christ to the world. Authentic Christian community is a place of honesty, vulnerability and opportunity—both to succeed and to fail. As we 'speak the truth in love' and hear it spoken (Ephesians 4:15–32), we are shaped by God.

This is not to say that interactions with others will be sunshine and roses when we share a common commitment to Christ. Romans 12:18 says, 'So far as it depends on you, live peaceably with all', making it clear that peace is not always possible and that living in peace takes effort. But in Christian community we can learn to talk about and accept our differences and to love one another in spite of them. Many of us will find it difficult to believe that God loves us until we experience love from others. At its best, the church offers us a place to be loved and accepted as we are.

And yes, experiencing that love does sometimes make a visible difference in us. Years ago, someone in my Sunday study class asked our group to help a woman who was in trouble. Trapped in an abusive marriage to an alcoholic husband, Jane (not her real name) struggled to get food for her children and to keep them safe. Class members began spending time with Jane's family. We played games with her children and made sure they had food. We assured Jane that God wanted better for her than she had. Eventually, she found strength to leave her husband. She began working part-time at the church, and it was obvious that she was an intelligent and capable woman. When I visited a few years later after moving away and Jane approached me in the hallway, I hardly recognised her. She was smiling, confident and relaxed, and she looked younger than when I first met her. She was working full-time with the church staff, her children doing well. Jane's entire life, even her appearance, changed because she came to know herself as loved by God. But it took being loved by a specific group of humans for her to come to believe it. Every group of believers has the potential and the power to become a community that loves people into freedom and wholeness.

Several meditations in this issue reflect the wonderful truth that we actually can love one another. You may want to re-read the meditations for May 2, 13, 15, 20, 30, and 31; June 4, 9, 12, 18, and 28; and July 17 before answering the reflection questions below.

Questions for Reflection

1. Read Hebrews 13:7. Who comes to mind as you reflect on this verse? How have you been shaped by knowing these people? How do you want to be like them?

2. Do you agree that we cannot believe that we are loved by God until we are loved by another person? Why or why not?

3. Is this article unrealistic about life among Christians? If so, how? If not, what experience makes you say that?

4. What has been the most important means by which God has shaped you? Through what relationships has God shaped you?

5. Do you know someone like Jane whose life has been greatly changed by relationship with God's people? If so, how did the change come about? If not, how do you connect to her story?

6. What is God saying to you through this article and your responses to it?

Mary Lou Redding

Don't forget to renew your annual subscription to *The Upper Room*! If you enjoy the notes, why not also consider giving a gift subscription to a friend or member of your family?

You will find a subscription order form on page 148.

The Upper Room is also available from your local Christian bookshop.

An Opportunity to Pray

Read Colossians 1:1–14

The prayer of a good person has a powerful effect.
James 5:16 (GNB)

'All inmates get down on the ground!' The pre-recorded message repeatedly blared from the guard tower. A man with a rifle scanned the compound from the tower window, ready to shoot. 'Officer needs assistance!' screamed the frantic voice over the two-way radio. Like ants pouring out of the ground, prison staff came running from every direction.

In the midst of this chaos, I calmly lay face down on the ground and prayed for the safety of the prison staff running by me, the inmates fighting in the distance, and the medical personnel en route. We needed divine intervention.

Opportunities to pray for the needs of others are all around us each day. We are not powerless; our prayers can alter the outcomes of situations. Prayer is a privilege God bestows on each of us. When we pray for others, we 'seek to do good to one another and to all' (1 Thessalonians 5:15, NRSV). Someone, somewhere needs our prayers. This is why the Bible tells us to pray for others. Who needs your prayers today?

Prayer: *Father, help us each day to pray for others and so express our love for them and for you. Amen*

Thought for the day: Prayer is an expression of love for God and neighbour.

Link2Life: *Keep a prayer list this month and look at it at month's end to see how situations have changed.*

Jeff Matthews (Indiana, US)

Orphaned

Read John 14:15–21

Jesus said, 'I will not leave you as orphans; I will come to you. Before long, the world will not see me any more, but you will see me. Because I live, you also will live. On that day you will realise that I am in my Father, and you are in me, and I am in you.'

John 14:18–20 (NIV)

Even though I was an adult when my parents died, I felt a keen sense of what it was like to be an orphan. Gone were the two people who had nurtured me and shaped my life. Sharp grief gave way to bewilderment: 'Who am I now? Who knows me deeply yet loves me anyway?' The Gospel of John recounts Jesus telling his disciples that although the time is coming that they will see him no more, he will always be a part of them, just as they will forever be part of him.

And so it has been with my parents. I see now that even after their deaths, their example of loving kindness continues to teach me and guide my life. That goes deeper than just warm memories. My parents are in me at a deep level, deeper than the mind can comprehend, as deep as the heart. And surely God was their heart's teacher.

In the same way, I come to know God through the life and love of Jesus. Nurturing that relationship through prayer and study, giving and serving, keeps me forever connected to the living God.

Prayer: *Gracious God, let who we are reflect who you are, in all that we do. Amen*

Thought for the day: Because of God's great love for us, we are never orphans.

Linda Tatum (North Carolina, US)

A Strong Example

Read Job 1:1–5, 2:1–9

Indeed we call blessed those who showed endurance. You have heard of the endurance of Job, and you have seen the purpose of the Lord, how the Lord is compassionate and merciful.
James 5:11 (NRSV)

The book of Job presents 'a man who was blameless and upright, one who feared God and turned away from evil' (Job 1:1). This book from the Bible was especially meaningful to me during the time when I was diagnosed with cancer and required surgery. I didn't know if the surgery would be successful or if it was too late. Thus it was important for me to keep peace in my heart, and the book of Job inspired me.

Until my experience with cancer, I thought I knew the book of Job well. But now reading it was different; I was reading the same words, but they were telling me a new story about physical pain and spiritual victory. I identified with Job, attacked on many fronts, and I decided to adopt his attitude. When the crisis threatened me, I read the Bible; and Job's example strengthened my spirit and helped me to overcome the pain and to survive.

This experience happened many years ago. The scars from the physical ordeal have disappeared. However, even today Job's example of refusing to give up on his relationship with God continues to help me in difficult situations.

Prayer: *Thank you, Lord, that every time we trust you and seek your help, you hear our prayers. Thank you for the wonderful examples of confidence and strong faith we discover in the Bible. Amen*

Thought for the day: In difficult situations, how can we trust and wait for God's help?

Antoaneta Petrova Kochevska (Pleven, Bulgaria)

Small Things with Huge Potential

Read Luke 13:18–19

A poor widow came and put in two small copper coins, which are worth a penny.

Mark 12: 42 (NRSV)

Matthew, Mark and Luke all relate this parable about the mustard seed, which Jesus used to describe the kingdom of heaven. The contrast between the tiny seed and the huge branching tree is so striking. I find it encouraging that Jesus told this story, as most of my days are now filled with small, commonplace actions. If I can offer any service to God at all it is on a limited scale; perhaps to exchange unexpected smiles with a stranger, or, in answer to an inner prompting, to ring someone and find that the call was urgently needed. But generally it is in the daily care of another. It isn't always easy to see these routine, sometimes menial jobs as a service to God.

But Jesus made it very clear that he placed value on the small and sometimes lowly task. He used the act of washing his disciples' feet to demonstrate his mission as the 'Servant King'. He drew the disciples' attention to the widow who put her tiny offering into the treasury. Jesus knew the true significance of her gift. He saw it against all the circumstances of her life and valued it not on its small financial level but on what the giving meant to her. I am convinced that Jesus, through the Holy Spirit, can use the least of our actions when they are done as though for him.

Prayer: *Dear Lord, when we feel discouraged and unappreciated, remind us that you value our smallest service. Amen*

Thought for the day: Give all you are able; God will make it grow.

Margaret Gregory (Hertfordshire, England)

Awesome Love

Read Mark 1:9–15

As Jesus was coming up out of the water, he saw heaven being torn open and the Spirit descending on him like a dove.
Mark 1:10 (NIV)

Summer storms on Florida's west coast can be intense and frightening. As scary as they may be, I still feel a curious sense of wonder as I observe these storms approaching. Seeing dark clouds angrily churning just before a deluge begins is a scene of beauty to me. Such a display is testimony to the awesome power of the One who created weather.

I imagine something similar when I think of the day at the Jordan River when Jesus was baptised. The scripture says that heaven was 'torn open'. This wasn't a gentle parting; rather, it was a powerful display to announce the anointing of God's Son, Jesus.

And yet what followed was a tender statement of love from a father to a son: 'You are my Son, whom I love; with you I am well pleased' (Mark 1:11). This same God who opened the heavens that day also reaches down to us in love. God is the all-powerful Lord who tenderly loves us and seeks our love in return. How can we resist or reject a love that is so awesomely, and yet gently, offered?

Prayer: *Kind Father, thank you for your amazing, undeserved and compelling love. Amen*

Thought for the day: No power on earth compares to the mighty love of God.

Michael J. Reynolds (Florida, US)

PRAYER FOCUS: THOSE WHO FEEL UNLOVABLE

Entangled in Sin

Read Psalm 40:1–3

He drew me up from the desolate pit, out of the miry bog, and set my feet upon a rock, making my steps secure.
Psalm 40:2 (NRSV)

As a child, I loved to spend long summer days running barefoot in our garden. Sometimes briars would take over sections of the garden; and because I did not want to tread on the thorns, I chose to run about elsewhere.

One day, I attempted to cross one of the briar patches. I tiptoed and hopped around, trying to avoid the thorns and thistles. After a few moments, I realised that I had made it only to the middle of the briar patch. My tender toes and I were surrounded. I felt trapped and afraid. Then I did the only thing I knew to do. I cried out, 'Daddy!' Soon, I saw my father running through the garden toward me. He picked me up and set my feet back on the soft grass.

Like me approaching that briar patch, we tiptoe around sin only to find ourselves suddenly entangled, with no way out. Fortunately, we have a loving father who hears our cry. God reaches down, pulls us out of the briars of sin and sets our feet on the right path.

Prayer: *Thank you, God, for saving us, as we pray, 'Our Father in heaven, hallowed be your name, your kingdom come, your will be done on earth as it is in heaven. Give us today our daily bread. Forgive us our debts, as we also have forgiven our debtors. And lead us not into temptation, but deliver us from the evil one.'* *

Thought for the day: When we get ourselves caught in a briar patch, God responds to our call for help.

Mitzi C. Smith (South Carolina, US)

PRAYER FOCUS: THOSE WHO ARE ENTANGLED IN SIN
* Matthew 6:9–13 (NIV)

Keeper of Crayons

Read Matthew 18:10–14

Even the hairs of your head are all counted.
Matthew 10:30 (NRSV)

My young son, Brindley, has autism, and one of the activities that soothes him is colouring. We often go to church with a notebook and crayons to keep him happy and occupied during the service. Brindley presses hard and can use up a box of crayons in a week or less. He wears his crayons down to small pieces. Some are less than half an inch in size, but he cherishes them no matter how little or worn down they are.

One Sunday morning, Brindley dropped his crayons on the floor. Of course, he immediately started to pick up his precious possessions. He was very careful to make sure he had accounted for all the crayons—every colour, every size, no matter how small or worn. To my son, each crayon mattered just as much as the other.

Brindley's attention to every single crayon is like God's love for each of us. God cares for us as separate individuals and has made us all different for a reason. In God's eyes we are all equally important and have a place in God's plan. We are always sought out and valued, one by one.

Prayer: *Heavenly Creator, help us to remember that you care for us even when we feel lost or insignificant. Thank you for loving us as we are. Amen*

Thought for the day: No matter what our size, shape, complexion or age is, each one of us matters to God.

Anjie Kokan (Wisconsin, US)

Training Opportunities

Read 2 Peter 1:2–8

Train yourself in godliness, for, while physical training is of some value, godliness is valuable in every way.
1 Timothy 4:7–8 (NRSV)

Recently I went to a gym. It was impressive! There was training equipment for every possible purpose to develop strength and endurance in back, legs, arms, chest, shoulders, thighs or any other muscles. The only thing missing was a personal trainer.

Having acquainted myself with the equipment, I looked around and noticed all kinds of people in the gym. Only one or two looked like the body builders I have seen in pictures. Some body shapes were thin; some were much heavier; and some were in between. They were of all ages, too—simply ordinary people who realised that it is a good idea to exercise for our health and physical well-being.

What I saw in the gym reminded me of the possibilities I have to do something for my spiritual health and well-being as well. God has given us many 'means of grace'—channels through which God helps us to develop in our Christian life. These include public worship, Bible study, Holy Communion, personal and community prayer and fasting, among others. When I need a personal trainer, I know I can find one in church or among experienced Christian friends.

Prayer: *Dear Lord, help us to care for both our physical and spiritual health. Amen*

Thought for the day: Just like our bodies, our spirits need regular nourishment.

Hans Vaxby (Moscow, Russia)

PRAYER FOCUS: FOR MORE DISCIPLINE IN PRAYER AND BIBLE READING   79

Like Moses

Read Joshua 1:1–9

The Lord said to Joshua, 'As I was with Moses, so I will be with you; I will never leave you nor forsake you.'
Joshua 1:5 (NIV)

One of my fears is public speaking. The bigger the audience, the more I fear. Sometimes this has prevented me from doing my best. One year at work, we made changes that required training for our staff across the country. Although I recognised this as an opportunity to challenge myself, I ignored it. I was content to assist while my manager conducted the training.

Then a request came from management for a retraining session. This time hundreds of people were to attend. I had no choice but to lead the training myself. I was terrified. After calming down, I spent time in prayer. I accepted my challenge and then reminded myself of a promise from Joshua 1:9, 'Be strong and courageous. Do not be terrified… for the Lord your God will be with you wherever you go.' Next, I prepared by reviewing the training material and practising my presentation. I went into the training, trusting in God.

God does not want us to stand on the sidelines of life. Instead, God asks us to face our fears, relying on divine strength. Fear of public speaking is only one battle; all of us have something that can terrify us. Whatever that is, we can remember that both the battle and the victory belong to the Lord.

Prayer: *Dear Father, thank you for the challenges that come our way. Teach us how to face our fears boldly and rely on you. Amen*

Thought for the day: God stands with us as we face our fears.

Libby Chacko (Pennsylvania, US)

Choice

Read 1 Peter 1:3–9

In his great mercy he has given us new birth into a living hope through the resurrection of Jesus Christ from the dead, and into an inheritance that can never perish, spoil or fade.

1 Peter 1:3–4 (NIV)

Tears coursed down Billy's face as his grazed knee was bathed, subsiding only when he was handed his comfort blanket.

My mind immediately flew back to a preacher I'd recently heard speak of comfort blankets. Then suddenly I was ten years old again, showing my uncle a picture I'd drawn. Without even a glance he turned away saying, 'Stop showing off.' His words had a profound effect on my life.

I've always been known as the quiet one in our family and for many years I hid behind that label; afraid to be anything else for fear of rejection or criticism. Shyness was my comfort blanket.

Until, that is, I realised that we can *choose* to cast off the negative. Jesus conquered all negativity on the cross. By placing our past hurts at his feet we can turn our back on them. The preacher's words, coupled with witnessing Billy's tears, brought home the truth of God's word. I realised that it was time to close the door on the negatives in my life. By handing them to Jesus, I could walk forward into a more positive, brighter tomorrow.

Prayer: *Lord, forgive us for hiding behind the 'comfortable'. Grant us the courage to step out and live in your freedom. Amen*

Thought for the day: The Lord is our Comforter.

Julia Cutting (East Yorkshire, England)

PRAYER FOCUS: THOSE WHO FIND IT DFFICULT TO LET GO OF THE PAST

Unconditional Love

Read Luke 5:27–32

Jesus said, 'I have not come to call the righteous, but sinners.'
Luke 5:32 (NIV)

Sometimes we all need a friend, someone who cares about us and our struggles. In fact, we do have someone to talk with who will not judge us but will unconditionally accept and love us. Scripture says that the tax gatherers and sinners came and sat down with Jesus. They felt comfortable coming and listening to him, perhaps because they knew he offered compassion and healing. As Jesus was both cleansing and making people whole, the Pharisees and scribes noticed and began to grumble. They complained that Jesus was receiving sinners and eating with them.

This is amazing! The pure, holy, spotless Lamb of God not only listened to impure, unrighteous sinners like me but touched them and ate with them.

We do not have to be discouraged by those around us today who are quick to judge and keep a record of our faults. Instead we can encourage ourselves and others with the truth that Christ is always ready with open arms to receive us and make us whole.

Prayer: *Thank you, Lord Jesus, that you accept us with unconditional love. Thank you for cleansing us and making us whole. Amen*

Thought for the day: Jesus came for sinners like you and me.

Michael D. Smith (South Carolina, US)

Remainders

Read John 6:1–13

Jesus told his disciples, 'Gather up the fragments that remain, that nothing be lost.'
John 6:12 (KJV)

My dreams, hopes and plans lay in ruins following my husband's death. I did not want to continue living. I didn't care to pick up the pieces of my life and go on.

In the midst of my grief, I happened upon the phrase 'getting meaning out of life's remainders'. Webster's dictionary defines 'remainder' as 'what is left after a part is taken away'. That surely described me following the loss of my husband of 55 years. Sometimes life leaves us with nothing but 'remainders'. The death of someone we love, damage to our reputation or a loss of employment can leave us feeling that we have nothing left to live for. However, Jesus teaches the importance of remainders in John 6:12, when he instructs his disciples, 'Gather up the fragments that remain, that nothing be lost.'

Just as Jesus was concerned with the fragments of food left after feeding the crowd, surely Christ is concerned that I do not waste the remaining time I have. It isn't always easy, but with God's help it is possible to get on with life and find purpose for our existence regardless of the losses we suffer.

Prayer: *God of love and power, hold us up when life hits us hard, and give us courage and strength to find new life in the face of grief. Thank you for staying with us all our days. Amen*

Thought for the day: Christ reminds us that our life is found in what we keep, not what we lose.

Dorothy C. Snyder (Tennessee, US)

PRAYER FOCUS: SOMEONE PICKING UP THE PIECES AFTER LOSS

Not Enough?

Read Matthew 15:29–39

Jesus looked at [the disciples] and said, 'For mortals it is impossible, but for God all things are possible.'
Matthew 19:26 (NRSV)

When I was asked to lead a Bible study on the book of Romans, I immediately thought that I didn't have enough knowledge or experience. But after a few weeks of study, lots of prayer and some help from my pastor, I began to see that I could lead the study and make it worthwhile and interesting for the people who attended. Like me, many of us when confronted with a task or asked to be in charge of a project lament that we do not have enough—enough help, enough money, enough time or enough talent.

The reaction of the disciples must have been similar when Jesus told them to feed the huge crowd with only seven loaves of bread and a few small fish. I can see them looking at each other, maybe rolling their eyes, and saying under their breath, 'This will never be enough to feed all these people.' Then when thousands had eaten their fill and the leftovers were gathered up, the disciples must have been astonished. However, they also must have realised that this was simply another example of the unlimited power of their Lord.

Sometimes we forget to consider this power. If we ask Christ for help in working for the kingdom, help is sure to come, and with God anything is possible. Instead of being discouraged when we think we don't have 'enough', we can decide to be open to the miraculous power of the Holy Spirit.

Prayer: *Lord, strengthen our trust in your power to help us work for you, even when we feel overwhelmed. Amen*

Thought for the day: God makes the impossible possible.

John R. Jackson (Delaware, US)

Greatness through Serving

Read 1 Peter 4:8–11

Who is greater, the one who is at the table or the one who serves? Is it not the one at the table? But I am among you as one who serves.
Luke 22:27 (NRSV)

After exploratory surgery, doctors concluded that my mother's sister, Dora, had a tumour in her stomach. Mum and I travelled to be with Dora and the family when surgery was performed to remove the tumour.

Later, after my aunt was settled in at home, family members took care of her, each with designated responsibilities. Mum's responsibility was praying with Aunt Dora and making her breakfast. When Mum wasn't up to doing that, I began to help.

One morning as I was preparing my aunt's breakfast, I suddenly realised what Jesus meant by his words in Luke 22:27, and to understand this Bible verse not just with my head but with my heart. I saw that we are to serve with a loving attitude. I admit that on the days I made Dora's breakfast, it wasn't always willingly. But I worked through that attitude by remembering that Jesus probably had times when he was weary and yet served those in need. He is my servant role model. Now I understand that true greatness is shown in committed service to others.

Prayer: *Lord, help us to serve those in need, those you send us. Help us always to serve with a loving heart. Amen*

Thought for the day: The great ones in God's kingdom are those who serve.

Jim Sanchez (Texas, US)

'Foolish' Faith

Read 1 Kings 17:8–16

'My thoughts are not your thoughts, neither are your ways my ways,' declares the Lord.
Isaiah 55:8 (NIV)

The coastline of Los Angeles faded as our ship sailed toward Brazil's western jungle frontier. We strongly believed that God wanted us to go to Brazil, but our friends were not convinced. 'Is this faith or foolishness?' they asked.

Walking by faith often invites accusations of foolhardiness. Consider Elijah's story. I can imagine how he felt when God sent him to a poor widow to supply him with food during a famine. Trusting God, Elijah asked the widow for bread. She replied that she had no bread—only a handful of flour and a little oil. She was going to use these in preparing the last meal for her son and herself. Doubt may have flashed into Elijah's mind, but God reassured them, 'The jar of flour will not be used up and the jug of oil will not run dry until the day the Lord gives rain on the land' (v. 14).

Elijah and the widow had to trust God for this miracle. And neither oil nor flour gave out. Again and again, God proved faithful.

Standing at the ship's rail, I realised that tests loomed ahead for us, too. But the God of Elijah is still the same. That trustworthy God would bring us through. And time showed that to be true.

Prayer: *God of change, who changes not, help us trust you even through tests of faith. Amen*

Thought for the day: To what 'foolish' task is God calling me today?

Mary D. MacKinnon (Paraná, Brazil)

Quietness in my Soul

Read Psalm 23

I do not concern myself with great matters... But I have stilled and quietened my soul.
Psalm 131:1–2 (NIV)

Our friends have a narrowboat. These boats were once used to carry coal and other essentials from town to town, along canals that criss-crossed the country. Whole families would live on the boats and work on them. Today the boats carry families on holiday instead.

Sitting on a narrowboat as it travels through the countryside at a maximum of four miles an hour, we experience things we miss completely when we race along by car or train—a bird alights beside us, the scent of flowers fills the air, frogs croak and fish jump. We are not rushing to get somewhere fast; we have time to think and meditate about life and the people around us.

I believe God wants me to stop rushing to get somewhere fast in my spiritual journey too; to be still and allow him to drop his quietness into my soul. It needs discipline to be still and quieten my soul, but it gives God a chance to speak and to breathe himself into my spirit.

Prayer: *Thank you, Lord, that you are eager to share yourself with me.*

Thought for the day: God has so much to show me on my way through the quiet places.

Marion Turnbull (Manchester, England)

PRAYER FOCUS: PEOPLE WHO ARE ALWAYS IN A HURRY

Making a Difference

Read John 2:1–11

To each one the manifestation of the Spirit is given for the common good.
1 Corinthians 12:7 (NIV)

As I walk to work in the cold and gloom of a midwinter early morning, I am cheered and heartened by the tiny points of colour provided by the few tough plants that continue to bloom. These plants include the odd rose on a bush that has not been pruned in readiness for spring, the occasional geranium that struggles to produce a single bloom, or the bright marigold out of sync with the rest of the garden.

This experience led me to recall times when I felt discouraged, as if my small efforts counted for nothing. We all tend to compare ourselves and what we do to others, and we decide that we are doing too little or that what we are doing is of little consequence. Yet there may be times when our efforts can be compared to the tiny points of colour on a winter's morning—they may be just what those we serve need to cheer them up, keep them going, or let them know that there is still life, colour and beauty around them.

Our efforts may be small, but that does not mean they are insignificant. God can use even the most ordinary people and actions to make a difference in someone's life. Turning the water into wine at the wedding at Cana may not be considered one of Jesus' bigger miracles; but it made a difference to the people who were present.

Prayer: *God of everything, thank you for the small joys and surprises of each day. Help us to be aware of you in the little and big moments of life. Help us to let our light shine for you. Amen*

Thought for the day: Imagine—God can use even me!

Meg Mangan (New South Wales, Australia)

Paid in Full

Read Romans 8:31–39

In [Christ] we have redemption through his blood, the forgiveness of our trespasses, according to the riches of his grace.
Ephesians 1:7 (NRSV)

I volunteer with a ministry that works with men who are moving back into society after serving prison sentences. These men were all convicted of crimes earlier in their lives and sent to prison. Some might consider the worst of their crimes to be unforgivable. Some of the men talk about how they have ruined their lives.

In the Bible, Peter's is a story of accepting God's grace and not dwelling on past failures. Peter was the leader of the disciples, and two New Testament books bear his name. But Peter committed what might be considered an unforgivable sin: on the night of Jesus' arrest, Peter denied knowing him. After the third denial, Peter realised what he had done and wept bitterly. However, because he remained open to Christ's message of grace and forgiveness, Peter moved past his failures and went on to do great things.

All the men in our prison ministry have made a decision to accept Christ. Rather than dwell on past failures, they have learned that Christ washed away their sins with his death on the cross. As Christians, no matter what our past failures, we can take heart in knowing that Jesus paid our debt in full.

Prayer: *Thank you, God, for forgiving all our sins because of what Jesus Christ has done for us. Amen*

Thought for the day: When we repent God forgives us, no matter what our sins are.

Link2Life: *Find a way to help the family of someone in prison.*

John D. Bown (Minnesota, US)

God Hears

Read Psalm 130:1–8

Out of the depths I cry to you, O Lord; O Lord, hear my voice. Let your ears be attentive to my cry for mercy.
Psalm 130:1–2 (NIV)

My husband and I own two breeder-chicken houses. As the hens were arriving, we had several equipment failures. When the feeder in one house broke, I started crying.

The next day, as I was walking through the chicken houses the birds were squawking and flying everywhere. Although the noise was loud, I still heard the cry of one chicken. Looking behind me, I saw a hen stuck in the feeder and gently freed her.

That made me think about the day before when I felt so overwhelmed. Sometimes I think no one cares and that even God does not hear me. But my being able to hear the one chicken among 12,000 others reminded me that amid all the chaos and noise of this world, God hears my cries. And God cares and comes to wipe away my tears.

The psalmist wrote that God's ears are attentive to our cries (Psalm 34:15). In our pain and frustration we often feel alone and lost, but God is always present to lift us up. God offers this mercy and peace to each of us, hearing our cries and responding to our needs.

Prayer: *Father God, thank you for hearing our cries. Continue to give us your peace as we face each challenge. Amen*

Thought for the day: No matter how loud the noise around us is, God always hears our cries.

Dell Skelton (Georgia, US)

The Privilege of Giving

Read 2 Corinthians 9:6–13

God is able to provide you with every blessing in abundance, so that by always having enough of everything, you may share abundantly in every good work.
2 Corinthians 9:8 (NRSV)

Once a week, I volunteer to drive adults who have medical appointments but do not have transport. Usually this is a pleasant and rewarding job, giving me the chance to meet and talk with people from many walks of life. However, occasionally the task can be quite demanding. One man is in a wheelchair. I drive him to the hospital, wheel him along a 200-yard corridor, take him up six floors in a lift, and deliver him to a dialysis unit where he receives treatment. Four hours later, I return and reverse the process to take him home.

Strange as it may seem, I relish this assignment. One reason is that ten years ago, I was saved from a similar plight when my kidneys failed. I was spared the burden of having to undergo dialysis three or four times a week because my wonderful daughter insisted on donating one of her kidneys to me.

I live now in certain awareness of what Jesus said was expected of those who receive great blessings. I have freedom, good health, a loving family, food and shelter. In gratitude, I take advantage of the chance to help others.

Prayer: *Gracious God, may we ever be conscious of the blessings you have given and willingly share them with others. Amen*

Thought for the day: We give to others because God has given to us.

Charles Levy (Ontario, Canada)

PRAYER FOCUS: FOR MORE ORGAN DONORS

Doors and Windows

Read Ephesians 3:14–21

To him who is able to do immeasurably more than all we ask or imagine, according to his power that is at work within us, to him be glory in the church and in Christ Jesus.
Ephesians 3:20–21 (NIV)

Having to accept mandatory retirement a few years ago from a university job that I loved, I felt a door had been closed for ever. I missed being around young people; I felt my daily interaction with them kept me young in thought and in spirit. Retirement has also become financially draining, which is why when God opened a window of opportunity for me to do supply teaching, I felt twice blessed.

I spend a lot of time on my knees now, both physically with the children and spiritually because of the children. I pray for them, for their parents and for those challenged with the responsibility of teaching them. I hadn't expected to begin my retirement this early; nor was this the way I had planned to spend it.

Change has definitely become harder for me as I have grown older. However, because my faith is strong, I am able to trust God and remain open and full of hope. Doing so has brought a life much fuller than anything I might have imagined and has also allowed me to meet my financial obligations.

Prayer: *Dear Lord, help us to discover our purpose and to live it in ways that bring us closer to you. Amen*

Thought for the day: What seems to us like an end can be God's door into a new beginning.

Anne Sheffield (Virginia, US)

Driving Safely

Read Proverbs 3:1–8

This God—his way is perfect; the promise of the Lord proves true; he is a shield for all who take refuge in him.
Psalm 18:30 (NRSV)

Early in the morning as I go to work, sometimes the fog is so dense that we drivers can hardly see anything. All that helps us are the lines on the road, emergency lights around accidents, and the signs that indicate the conditions ahead. What would happen if we did not have these helps to drive safely? Maybe we would not reach our destination or we would suffer more accidents.

In a similar way, I see that God uses scripture to show us the path we are to take. The Bible is full of advice for each situation we may confront in our daily living. For instance, Paul advises: 'So far as it depends on you, live peaceably with all' (Romans 12:18). 'A soft answer turns away wrath, but a harsh word stirs up anger' (Proverbs 15:1) is another good piece of advice. The Teacher in Ecclesiastes tells us: 'Though one might prevail against another, two will withstand one. A threefold cord is not quickly broken' (4:12) and: 'Much study is a weariness of the flesh' (12:12).

We can choose whether to live according to our own will or to follow the Bible's advice.

Prayer: *Teach us, God, to trust in you, to follow your ways, and to live according to your will. Amen*

Thought for the day: God's word offers us daily guidance.

Magdalena Alvarado (Coahuila, Mexico)

Answering the Call

Read Luke 10:25–37

'Which of these three, do you think, was a neighbour to the man who fell into the hands of the robbers?' [The lawyer] said, 'The one who showed him mercy.' Jesus said to him, 'Go and do likewise.'
Luke 10:36, 37 (NRSV)

At an early age, I began to spend Saturdays working in my father's business. Once when I was about 12, my father and I left work late in the afternoon, tired and eager to go home. On our way to the car, we noticed an elderly man across the street slip on some ice and fall. Without hesitation, my father led me across the street, where we helped the man to his feet. He was conscious but bleeding from some scrapes and a cut on his nose. We helped him back to his small flat and spent about an hour with him, cleaning his face and bandaging his nose. We listened as he spoke of the loneliness and despair in his life. Now in my 50s, I often reflect on this occasion and how special it made me feel to comfort someone in pain.

God calls us to take advantage of opportunities to show love and compassion to those in need. Much of what I learned from my father centred on hard work and disciplined pursuit of our goals. But that day he taught me the importance of detouring from our plans and reaching out to a person in need.

Prayer: *Dear God, break through the din of our routines so that we may hear the cry of those who are struggling and find ways to extend to them your love and friendship. Amen*

Thought for the day: The most important task God has for us today may not be on our to-do list.

Joe Green (Minnesota, US)

Eyes that See

Read 2 Kings 6:8–17

Elisha prayed, 'O Lord, open his eyes so he may see.' Then the Lord opened the servant's eyes.

2 Kings 6:17 (NIV)

In today's reading, Dothan was about to be attacked and Elisha's servant was panicking; he didn't understand why Elisha was calm. The difference between them was that Elisha could see God's power. After Elisha had prayed, the servant was able to see what Elisha had been seeing—the army of God surrounding the attackers. The enemy no longer seemed so overwhelming.

How often am I like that servant—falling prey to fear and anxiety, feelings that are unfounded or are as nothing when compared to God's power? In the last few years, I have felt attacked from multiple directions. My job has been at risk; work relationships and redundancies have been stressful; my parents were diagnosed with cancer, and my children made some bad choices when faced with temptations. But through it all, we have seen God's amazing power. I still have a job, my parents are cancer survivors, and our children are now making better decisions about their lives. When I open my eyes to the amazing power of God, I have no fear.

Prayer: *God, grant us eyes that see your power all around us so that we do not fear enemies in this world. Amen*

Thought for the day: Do I act as if I see God's power?

Russell E. Denslow (Florida, US)

PRAYER FOCUS: THOSE STRUGGLING TO SEE GOD'S POWER

Whole Again

Read Romans 3:21–26

I am the Lord your God, the holy God of Israel, who saves you.
Isaiah 43:3 (GNB)

Some months after I had been appointed to my first student pastorate, I was struggling to complete my Sunday sermon. My youngest daughter, Christina, came into the room with her favourite cloth doll. The stitching around its arms and legs was frayed, and the seams were coming apart. With sadness in her eyes, she asked if I would sew the arms and legs back together. I said to Christina, 'Daddy is busy working on his sermon. I'll sew up your doll later.' She walked slowly out of the room.

As I began putting the finishing touches on my sermon, I looked up from my desk. Christina was back in the room and with sad eyes asked me again to mend her doll. Guilt got the better of me, and I asked her to give me the doll. I got out the sewing kit and began to mend one of the arms. As I did so, God seemed to speak to me. 'Before you knew of my love and saving grace, you were much like this doll—torn and broken. Your life was coming apart. But because I love you, I have put your life back together. In love, I have made you whole.'

That night, both Christina and I were blessed by the love of God—who sees our weak, torn lives and makes us whole again.

Prayer: *Merciful God, thank you for loving us even though we don't deserve it. Amen*

Thought for the day: God sees our brokenness through eyes of love and works to make us whole again.

John I. Penn (Georgia, US)

Family History

Read Matthew 20:1–13

To all who received him, who believed in his name, he gave the right to become children of God.
John 1:12 (NIV)

I've always been hypersensitive to medication. We first discovered this when, as young children, my older sister and I both went to the hospital at the same time for tonsillectomies. We shared a room; my sister's bed was next to the window. Soon we were given injections to prepare us for surgery. Beverly immediately became drowsy, but my reaction was to sing loudly and declare I wanted to fly out of the window! Bev begged our mum to make me be quiet so she could sleep. We laugh often about that incident and have passed it on as a part of our family history.

Like my sister and me with medication, people react differently to the message of God's love. One person might listen attentively and immediately decide to follow Christ. Another might weigh the truth for many years before believing. Our responsibility is to talk about how God has changed us and how God assures us of eternal life. But we cannot make the decision for others; we all have free will.

Just as my mum couldn't control my reaction to that medicine, we cannot control how others respond to the truth of God's love. But we share that love, knowing that our God cherishes our uniqueness yet cares for each of us the same.

Prayer: *O God, give us holy boldness to speak about Christ to others so they can come to know and believe in you. Amen*

Thought for the day: Each of us responds uniquely to Christ and to the call to follow him.

Janet Flicker Moore (North Carolina, US)

Direction Signs

Read Psalm 119:105–112
Your word is a lamp to my feet and a light to my path.
Psalm 119:105 (NRSV)

During my recent visit to the United States, I had to travel from Chicago to St Louis. I reached the airport on time; but instead of looking at the direction signs to get to my flight, I sought guidance from a person, one who sent me off in the wrong direction. When I finally found the way I needed to go, I had very little time to reach the plane. Confused, I prayed and then followed the signs displayed for my flight. I reached the plane shortly before take-off.

In a similar way in life, we reach our ultimate goal by following the direction signs clearly written in the word of God. One direction given in scripture became clear to my wife and me recently. As we were enthusiastically planning the future of our family, what we would do and where we would go, the scripture verse in my morning devotion spoke to me: 'You do not even know what tomorrow will bring. What is your life? For you are a mist that appears for a little while and then vanishes' (James 4:14). I learned to seek God's help as I plan. I am not the boss of my life; God is. And God is always faithful and good and right.

Prayer: *Lead us, O God, in the ways we should go. Teach us to watch for your direction and to follow your guidance. Amen*

Thought for the day: God is supposed to be our trip planner, not our baggage handler.

Zafar Iqbal (Punjab, Pakistan)

An Earful of Prayer

Read 1 Thessalonians 5:16–24
Pray without ceasing.
1 Thessalonians 5:17 (NRSV)

Have you ever had a song stuck in your head—one that continues to play over and over in your mind? Since I've participated in church choirs starting when I was small, I have a huge memory collection of anthems and hymns I have sung. When reading the Bible, I often come across a passage that was used as a lyric in one of those songs. I wind up singing the song to myself, and then it gets stuck in my head—which means I sing it over and over until it drives me almost crazy. There's even a term in English for this phenomenon: earworm.

However, when I recently came across the verse, 'Pray without ceasing' in 1 Thessalonians 5, I wondered if those earworms might actually be good for me. If I sing the same spiritual song over and over, couldn't that be considered continuous prayer? The words of those songs certainly turn my mind toward God, as I conduct my daily, worldly business.

Now when a song I know from church gets stuck in my head, I pay attention to what I'm singing, using the words as a prayer rather than trying to push the song from my mind. Plus, I listen more attentively to what God might be trying to tell me through that particular song. An earworm can become a blessing!

Prayer: *Lord, help us to pray without ceasing and to keep our minds focused on you. Amen*

Thought for the day: How can I pray without ceasing?

Link2Life: *Listen to some music that inspires you to praise God.*

Kim Sheard (Virginia, US)

PRAYER FOCUS: SOMEONE LEARNING ABOUT PRAYER

Cling to God!

Read 2 Kings 18:1–7

[Hezekiah] held fast to the Lord; he did not depart from following him but kept the commandments that the Lord commanded Moses.
2 Kings 18:6 (NRSV)

When my son was about three years old, I brought him along with me to a men's group meeting at church. At the start of the meeting, I noticed how closely my son was sitting next to me. In an unfamiliar place, surrounded by a room full of strange and therefore probably scary-looking men, he felt frightened and insecure. So he held on tightly to the only familiar person in that room—his father. As long as Dad was near, he felt safe.

The way he clung to me made me think about the importance of our clinging to God. 2 Kings 18 describes Hezekiah as a righteous king. He was successful and prosperous. But more important, Hezekiah clung to the Lord. I believe that is the secret in unleashing spiritual power in our lives.

Clinging to God may sound simple, but it's not as easy as it may seem. Humans have a propensity to be independent. After sitting close for about 30 minutes, my son slowly loosened his grip on me as he became more comfortable. But when we become comfortable spiritually, we may begin to depend on ourselves and our abilities and loosen our grip on God. We find ourselves working more and praying less. The secret to unleashing spiritual power in our lives is to maintain constant dependence on God—clinging to God as if our life depended on it, never letting go.

Prayer: *Dear Lord, teach us to cling to you as a child holds fast to its parent and to not let go. Amen*

Thought for the day: Cling to God; your life depends on it.

Marc Villa-Real (Antipolo City, Philippines)

Coincidences?

Read Psalm 33:12–19

The eyes of the Lord are on those who fear him, on those whose hope is in his unfailing love.
Psalm 33:18 (NIV)

Our dining table had languished unused for 20 years. Since our children had grown up and moved out, we decided to rearrange the furniture to fit our new situation. Throwing out our old kitchen table and replacing it with the more stylish table from the dining room was significant for us.

The next Monday morning, I fell down the stairs, broke my leg and dislocated my ankle. Having moved the table, we had room for my bed to be downstairs for two months while my leg was in plaster.

I needed quite a lot of assistance, especially for the first few weeks. People phoned to offer help, saying, for example, 'I can come round, but only on Wednesday. Would that be of any help?' On seven consecutive occasions, the days offered were exactly the days when my husband would be away travelling for work. I saw these not as coincidences but as God at work.

I heard a voice inside me say, 'I love you so. Do not be anxious. I've sent many dear friends and relatives to help you.' I began to understand. I know God didn't make me fall, but I believe he provided for me in specific and detailed ways to help me as I recovered.

Prayer: *Thank you, loving God, for watching over us in difficult situations. Amen*

Thought for the day: Look for God's hand in your life. How has God cared for you?

Link2Life: *Help someone who has had surgery or is ill.*

M.S. Foster (Cheshire, England)

PRAYER FOCUS: THOSE RECOVERING FROM INJURIES

A Dark and Stormy Night...

Read Luke 8:22–25

[Nothing] in all creation, will be able to separate us from the love of God in Christ Jesus our Lord.
Romans 8:39 (NRSV)

My daughter cried out in the night, afraid of the storm. Thunder boomed and lightning flashed. She said she was afraid that the wind might sweep her away in the darkness. I tried to comfort her as the windows rattled and the wind howled against the house.

That night, I could understand what the disciples felt as a storm came upon them on the Sea of Galilee and their boat was beginning to be tossed by the waves (see Mark 4:35–41 and Luke 8:22–25). Now, as then, only Jesus Christ can give us peace in the midst of a storm. If we call on his name and remember the assurances in scripture, it will give us courage in the midst of all adversity.

As I told my daughter, 'The best thing about storms is that they always pass.' And each of us can always pray, as my daughter and I did that night.

Prayer: *Heavenly Father, thank you for simple prayers and the peace you give when we are afraid of the storm. We pray as Jesus taught us, saying, 'Father, hallowed be your name, your kingdom come. Give us each day our daily bread. Forgive us our sins, for we also forgive everyone who sins against us. And lead us not into temptation.'* Amen*

Thought for the day: Even amid raging storms, God offers us courage and peace.

Vince H. Byrd (Georgia, US)

Take Time to Enjoy

Read Genesis 1:31—2:3

This is what the Sovereign Lord, the Holy One of Israel, says: 'In repentance and rest is your salvation, in quietness and trust is your strength.'
Isaiah 30:15 (NIV)

Every Monday morning, a to-do list stares up at me from my calendar. Gone is the sense of accomplishment from the previous week and its completed tasks. A new list of tasks awaits me, including some items that didn't get done the previous week (or the week before that) and have been moved to the current week's list.

At the beginning of the week, I often find myself trying to accomplish several tasks on my list in a single day. I enjoy the sense of accomplishment that comes from rapidly checking items off my list. But I also feel stressed and exhausted from trying to do too much too quickly. I have to remind myself to slow down, to remember that I don't have to accomplish everything in a single day.

God could have created the earth and the vast universe in a single day or even a single moment. But he didn't do it that way. Why? Could it be that God wanted to stop and enjoy each piece of creation as it was being created? God also chose to rest on the seventh day, to enjoy the completed work.

God is teaching me to seek balance between work and rest. God is also helping me to realise that slowing down and enjoying life is as important as checking off a completed item from my list.

Prayer: *Creator God, teach us to enjoy the journey as much as reaching the destination. In Jesus' name we pray. Amen*

Thought for the day: Savour each moment as a gift from God.

Janine A. Kuty (Virginia, US)

Know your Neighbours

Read Mark 12:28–34

The whole law is summed up in a single commandment, 'You shall love your neighbour as yourself.'
Galatians 5:14 (NRSV)

Eleven years ago we moved into a new neighbourhood. My wife and I discussed how we might reach out in love to the 25 families who live on our short road. Our first thought was, 'Where should we begin?' We gathered names and addresses, and agreed to pray for each person every day. We believe that we need to talk to God about our neighbour before we talk to our neighbour about God.

Soon we began to invite one family at a time into our home for a meal and to get to know each other. Our prayer was for each person in our community to sense God's presence. We sent cards and notes at special times, and we remained vigilant for incidents of need or crisis. We watched for new families and took a freshly baked loaf of bread to them, welcoming them as neighbours.

Today we rejoice in the open doors God has given us and for the privilege of loving our neighbours through daily prayers. We also praise God for opportunities to serve and for the relationships we have with these people. What better way to 'love our neighbours as ourselves' than to pray God's blessing upon each, day by day?

Prayer: *Loving God, help us to be instruments of your love to those who live around us. In Jesus' name we pray. Amen*

Thought for the day: We do God's work when we pray for and love our neighbours.

Link2Life: *Get to know your neighbours so that you can pray for their specific needs.*

John M. Drescher (Pennsylvania, US)

The Right Treasure

Read Matthew 6:19–21

Store up riches for yourselves in heaven.
Matthew 6:20 (GNB)

Like many people, I sometimes worry about how we are going to survive in the current economic situation. In tough times, we may turn to possessions for comfort and enjoyment; sometimes in order to feel better we even spend money that we don't have.

I was reminded of this recently in church when I noticed a stranger in the pew ahead of me. He was dirty and unkempt, and he listened intently to the sermon and sang the hymns joyfully. When the offertory plate came around, I saw him drop in a few coins. He gave without hesitation.

Often we who are more fortunate than that man don't tithe, don't spend time with God regularly, don't give of our time or money to help the poor and homeless. Too often we don't offer a kind word to a stranger, take time to chat with a lonely person, or spend an hour a week to help at a soup kitchen.

I have decided to stop using so much of my time building up treasures on earth so that I can more faithfully live out God's word.

Prayer: *Dear God, help us to carry out your word faithfully, for the benefit of those you love. Amen*

Thought for the day: Live your life so people can see God's love in your actions.

Shaun McHardy (Cape Town, South Africa)

PRAYER FOCUS: NEWCOMERS TO MY CHURCH

The Special Gift of Time

Read 2 Corinthians 13: 4

The Lord will fulfil his purpose for me; your love, O Lord, endures for ever.
Psalm 138:8 (NIV)

As I closed the door to the last of my brood to start their working lives, my mind was in turmoil. This was supposed to be the defining moment when my life changed. Now I could begin to pay real attention to deepening my spiritual life by taking a more hands-on approach.

But at the back of my mind was the diagnosis given to me recently by my GP. I had multiple sclerosis. How was it going to affect my future activities?

That was several years ago. In that time I have come to realise that God has a purpose for all of us, whether we are fully active or housebound. I have a very special gift from God, and that is time, so precious in this busy world of ours. Time to study the Bible, to write letters of comfort, and above all to pray. Today, I have a very busy Christian life. Everyone, no matter what their circumstances, can forward God's work.

Prayer: *Dear God, help us to remember that when we feel weak, you will make us strong to serve you. Amen*

Thought for the day: God has a purpose for everyone—and for me.

Link2Life: *Open the pages of your newspaper and pray for the people you read about.*

Barbara Baalham (Suffolk, England)

Under Construction

Read Jeremiah 18:1–6

Suffering produces endurance, and endurance produces character, and character produces hope, and hope does not disappoint us.
Romans 5:3–5 (NRSV)

I stood at the building site of our church's mission house as the stonemasons worked. The house began to take shape as they skilfully arranged the cement blocks. From time to time, the masons intentionally chiselled away a chunk of the well-moulded, rectangular cement blocks before they laid them.

Initially, I thought they were wasting precious resources. I wondered, 'If they knew that they were going to chisel away some of the blocks, why didn't they make them smaller from the beginning?' As I watched, I realised that they were chiselling the blocks to give the building's facade character.

This observation gave me a better understanding of the story of the potter and the clay in Jeremiah 18:1–6. Sometimes, the circumstances and challenges we face in life almost destroy us. These can in fact produce in us shape and character that we will need to face life. However my experiences chisel me, I want to learn to accept God's work of moulding me.

Prayer: *Lord, when life's circumstances challenge us, teach us to accept your direction. Help us to remember that all things can be used for good. Amen*

Thought for the day: God is at work in us to give us life.

Francis Lawer Sackitey (Eastern Region, Ghana)

In Spite of Loss

Read James 1:1–4

Precious in the sight of the Lord is the death of his faithful ones.
Psalm 116:15 (NRSV)

The message said to telephone; I knew it would be news that I did not want to hear. Our loved one had died. We were sad, angry and simply didn't understand. Although we had thought she might not win her battle, her death didn't make sense. Why her? She was strong, vibrant and young—only 36 years old.

During her illness, I kept turning to the book of James and the book of Job. James teaches us about trials in our life; Job was a man who faced great loss and yet trusted God. The first chapter of James says, 'Whenever you face trials of any kind, consider it nothing but joy, because you know that the testing of your faith produces endurance' (vv. 2–3).

In times of grief, it's easy to ask why. But as I thought more about my family's loss, I began to think of the many blessings God has given us. I realised that what matters is loving one another in whatever time we have. Our loved one was ready to meet God; her relationship with the Lord was strong. That knowledge gave our family peace—and even joy—in spite of our loss.

Prayer: *Dear God, in times of grief, help us to lean on your word. Strengthen us to know what is most important—our relationship with you. Amen*

Thought for the day: God strengthens us in times of loss.

Byron R. Samuels (Florida, US)

Wrapped in Prayer

Read Philippians 4:4–9

Do not worry about anything, but in everything by prayer and supplication with thanksgiving let your requests be made known to God.
Philippians 4:6 (NRSV)

Knitting brings me a sense of peace and renewal. Even though I only know one basic stitch, I can knit any number of pieces, especially scarves. Though the particular pieces vary, the stitch I use doesn't. Once I have the number of stitches set on my needle, I can just knit away without having to think about what I am doing.

At our church, a group of women gets together once a month to knit. These women taught me how to make a prayer shawl — which has quickly turned out to be my favourite piece to knit. As we knit the shawls, we pray for those who will receive them. When they wrap themselves in the prayer shawl, they wrap themselves in our prayer and care.

I give thanks for the person who began this prayer shawl ministry because it helps all of us to do something good for others. My knitting also takes me out of the world's hectic pace and into a time of peace, where my strength is renewed by God's Spirit working among us.

Prayer: *Thank you, Lord, for giving us peace as we work toward helping others. Thank you for the opportunities you give us to be a part of your work in their lives. Amen*

Thought for the day: We find God's peace when we help others.

Susie Hoffmann (Ohio, US)

Uneven Ways

Read Psalm 106:1–15

Commit your way to the Lord; trust in him, and he will act.
Psalm 37:5 (NRSV)

The road from the Luanda airport to southern Angola is under repair. Clearing away the old road's surface to allow the repairs has left the road below the level of the surrounding buildings, making it difficult for the pedestrians to get to the banks, shops and markets along the way. I found myself wondering if we could lower the buildings a little, or somehow raise the road surface to be level with them.

While the work of fixing the road goes on, people continue to step up and down every day between the level of the road and the level of the buildings. In the midst of the upheaval and the noise of the heavy machines, they wait for the day when the work will be completed, providing more comfortable travel.

This uneven and challenging area reminds me of the story of the Israelites after they crossed the Red Sea. In spite of their disobedience, God led them through the wilderness and delivered them from the hands of their enemies.

The road of life is difficult and sometimes full of twists. Sometimes we have to go up and to go down, go to the right and the left. We pass through valleys and climb mountains. Meanwhile, the Lord looks after us during our journey and leads us no matter what part of the path we face each day.

Prayer: *Our God and guide, strengthen us and give us the hope that will enable us to overcome life's difficulties. We trust you. Amen*

Thought for the day: In life's ups and downs, God journeys with us.

Emilio J.M. de Carvalho (Luanda, Angola)

A Leap of Faith

Read Matthew 13:18–23

Give, and it will be given to you. A good measure, pressed down, shaken together, running over, will be put into your lap; for the measure you give will be the measure you get back.
Luke 6:38 (NRSV)

As I watched two squirrels jump from branch to branch and tree to tree, I marvelled at how the next branch always held the squirrels' weight. When the branches dipped, the squirrels held on. Amazed, I realised that they must know instinctively how far they can jump. I wish I had that same skill when it comes to personal decisions.

In these uncertain economic times, our church has been falling short of what we usually receive in offerings. After prayer, my husband and I talked about whether we could give more. Unlike those squirrels that seemed to know how far they could leap, I hesitated to jump ahead with a promise to increase our giving.

Then we reasoned: with our past level of giving, God has always continued to meet our needs. Why should we fear future giving? We don't need to worry about taking another leap of faith. God has given us enough that we can give to others.

Prayer: *Heavenly Father, forgive us when we fear giving back to you what is yours to begin with. Help us always to give to you with a cheerful heart. Amen*

Thought for the day: Our true security is found not in money but in God's eternal love.

Deb Vellines (Illinois, US)

PRAYER FOCUS: TO GIVE WITH GREATER TRUST AND JOY

Life in the Spirit

Read Galatians 5:16–26
Live by the Spirit, and you will not gratify the desires of the sinful nature.
Galatians 5:16 (NIV)

Since my daughter turned two, we have been on a journey with the Lord. We started walking to a small church down the road and have gone almost every Sunday since. We tramp through the snow to church on winter days; we ride bicycles in the summer. How rewarding this has been for us! Our relationships with God have blossomed like flowers.

In those early years, however uplifting morning worship was, darkness encased my heart. I started my days resolved to live in God's light and finished in the darkness of a pub, in an alcoholic haze. I took the contradiction of my life to the Lord in prayer, but my anger and frustration increased. One day in an argument with my wife, rage overcame me and I punched a hole in the wall of our home. A painful separation from my wife and daughter ensued.

But God has blessed me with a strong, caring, forgiving wife; and God has answered my prayers for sobriety. During that separation and to this day, I have tried to live Galatians 5:22–23: 'The fruit of the Spirit is love, joy, peace, patience, kindness, goodness, faithfulness, gentleness and self control.'

My days are consistent now. No longer is each day a contradiction of light and darkness. My family laughs and loves. The Lord has truly blessed our home.

Prayer: *Lord, we pray for peace that can be found only in your love. Help us to overcome our sinful nature and its desires. Amen*

Thought for the day: In the love of God we find our peace.

Robbie Wisniewski (New Jersey, US)

What Really Matters

Read Mark 2:1–12

God is faithful; by him you were called into the fellowship of his Son, Jesus Christ our Lord.
1 Corinthians 1:9 (NRSV)

Like most of the people I know, I was taught early in life that with enough hard work and dedication, I could reach any goal. I never considered myself a bad person; but because I learned to concentrate all my efforts on material success, I neglected my spiritual development. Though I attended church, I had no relationship at all with God.

All this changed in 2003, when I suddenly developed epilepsy. I was unable to work or even to drive. Overnight, my world changed dramatically. My wife and I were at the point of losing everything we had worked our whole lives for, with nowhere to turn and no one to turn to. At this low point in our lives, the members of the church we attended came to our rescue. They drove me to doctors' appointments and wrote letters on my behalf. Most importantly, they provided my wife and me with a spiritual and emotional refuge, along with offering practical help during the storms we were facing.

I am still disabled, and the life I knew for many years is over. However, I have learned that what really matters in life is not personal gain but faith and trust in God.

Prayer: *Loving God, always give us the faith to do your will and to trust you in the storms of life. Amen*

Thought for the day: Christian community makes God's love real.

Mark A. Carter (Texas, US)

A New Home

Read John 14:1–4

Jesus said, 'I am going there to prepare a place for you.'
John 14:2 (NIV)

My mum and dad moved from New Jersey to live near us in Florida. In the weeks leading up to my parents' arrival, my husband and I worked tirelessly getting their new house ready for them. As we cleaned and painted, I remembered what Jesus said about going to prepare a place for us so that where he is we also will be.

We prepared an earthly home for my parents, but Jesus prepares our eternal home so that we may always be with him. This home will endure for ever. As Paul wrote, 'No eye has seen, no ear has heard, no mind has conceived what God has prepared for those who love him' (1 Corinthians 2:9).

Even more than I love my parents, God loves us more. Our destination and final home is with our Creator.

Prayer: *We praise you, Father, for always taking care of us, here on earth and in eternity. As Jesus taught us, we pray, 'Our Father which art in heaven, Hallowed be thy name. Thy kingdom come. Thy will be done in earth, as it is in heaven. Give us this day our daily bread. And forgive us our debts, as we forgive our debtors. And lead us not into temptation, but deliver us from evil: For thine is the kingdom, and the power, and the glory, for ever. Amen.'* *

Thought for the day: God is preparing a place for each of us in eternity.

JoAnn Decker (Florida, US)

* Matthew 6:9–13 (KJV)

The Words we Choose

Read Hebrews 4:12–16

We speak of these things in words not taught by human wisdom but taught by the Spirit.
1 Corinthians 2:13 (NRSV)

Often when I write, I struggle to find the right word to express my thoughts. A dictionary can help, but I find that a thesaurus is especially useful because it groups words of similar meaning. The thesaurus helps me find the word that most closely says what I want to convey and allows me to move on with my writing.

Sometimes we face struggles in our lives or the lives of others, and we find ourselves looking for what to do or say. At these times the Bible is a valuable resource that will guide us. The more familiar we become with the Bible, the more quickly we can find words that will inspire us and others with God's love and lead us to the right course of action—whether in word or deed. Often the book of Psalms or Jesus' words in the gospels are a great place to start. Meditations like those in *The Upper Room* often guide us to scripture passages that present the exact word we need for the struggles we or others are facing.

Prayer: *Dear God, help us replace negative words and thoughts with your words of hope, joy and peace that we can find in scripture. Amen*

Thought for the day: Caring words can bring God's light and hope.

Mark H. Anderson (Pennsylvania, US)

God is my Blanket

Read Psalm 32

You are a hiding place for me; you preserve me from trouble; you surround me with glad cries of deliverance.
Psalm 32:7 (NRSV)

While on the train to St Petersburg, I saw a touching scene. A father, mother and young child were travelling in the neighbouring compartment. Toward evening, the train became cold. The mother and child had fallen asleep, so the father took a warm blanket and carefully covered his wife and child. At that moment I remembered the Russian translation of Psalm 32:7, 'God is my blanket.'

What does this mean for me? A mother swaddles her child. A grandson lovingly puts a blanket over his grandmother who has fallen asleep in her armchair. In the pouring rain, someone offers a place under an umbrella. When one spouse has fallen asleep from exhaustion, the other tenderly covers him or her with a blanket. When a person is weak and old and in a hospital bed, another pulls up blankets to keep the elderly person warm.

We may not notice these blankets, and other 'blankets' of concern that people offer us, believing that we are alone and that God is indifferent to us. But scripture tells us that from the day of our birth to the end of our earthly days, the Lord covers us with care, mercy, warmth and love.

Prayer: *When we are especially vulnerable and defenceless, thank you, God, for covering us with your care and giving us new life. Help us to remember and to shield and warm others with your love. Amen*

Thought for the day: Our attention and concern can convey God's loving care to those near us.

Natalya Ilyushonok (Grodnenskaya, Belarus)

The Journey Ahead

Read Hebrews 12:1–3

When Jesus spoke again to the people, he said, 'I am the light of the world. Whoever follows me will never walk in darkness, but will have the light of life.'
John 8:12 (NIV)

Late one afternoon, I set out to drive to my parents' home. I was tired when I began the journey, and the sun was beginning to set. I found myself focusing on the horizon as far as I could see, and I felt overwhelmed by the thought of how many miles I still had to travel. I realised that I needed to shift my focus to the patch of road directly in front of my car, taking the journey one mile at a time.

I have experienced this same challenge in my faith journey. Often, instead of being faithful in the tasks right in front of me, I find myself concentrating on the destination, wondering how I am going to get there rather than seeking the One who is going to get me there. When I have focused on worshipping God and seeking Christ, God often has shown me the next step. The times when I have been faithful to take that one step, the next step became apparent, and then the next, and soon I was looking back over my path to see how God had brought me to a new place.

As Christians, we have a long journey ahead of us. How do we get to where we are going? We focus our eyes on Christ, and he lights our path—one step at a time.

Prayer: *Lord Jesus, help us to wait on you to reveal our next step. Amen*

Thought for the day: Focus your eyes on Christ rather than the journey ahead.

Kristin Evans (Tennessee, US)

PRAYER FOCUS: SAFETY FOR TRAVELLERS

Buzz like a Bee

Read Matthew 28:16–20

Go… and make disciples of all nations, baptising them in the name of the Father and of the Son and of the Holy Spirit.
Matthew 28:19 (NRSV)

When we speak about bees, most people automatically think of stings or of honey. However sweet honey may taste, making it is not the primary purpose of bees. The most important function of bees is pollinating plants. Farmers here in South Africa rely on bees to pollinate almost 70 different crops. Hives are often imported and situated close to fields for this specific purpose. Around the world, bees fill this important role.

There is similarity between bees and us in our Christian walk. The Crusades and other examples in history show that, unfortunately, the Church has sometimes caused pain in the name of Christ. We've also all benefited in one way or another from the good the Church has done and the sweetness of relationship with God.

Perhaps there is a greater lesson for us—that the main purpose of being a follower of Christ is to 'pollinate' the world with the gospel of love and peace by our personal, living example.

Prayer: *Dear God, when we become complacent, remind us that we are salt and leaven and light and that our purpose is to season and enrich the world with your love. Amen*

Thought for the day: Who near me needs to hear Christ's gospel of peace and love and see it lived out?

Roland P. Rink (Gauteng, South Africa)

Without Asking

Read Ruth 1:1–18
Ruth said to Naomi, 'Wherever you go, I will go.'
Ruth 1:16 (TEV)

On a brisk November morning at a tiny hospital, my mother lay in the intensive-care unit, gravely ill. A doctor sat down with my infant son and me in the waiting room. He fumbled with his pen as he cleared his throat. Then he explained that my mum was 'a very, very ill lady' and that I shouldn't expect her to survive.

After he left, I didn't move. I just kept holding my son close and listening to the sounds outside the door. I heard the lift doors opening and closing around the corner. I heard people talking and laughing and scurrying from one place to another. It was just another busy day for many other people.

Couldn't everyone see that the entire world had just stopped? My mother was dying!

Then my phone rang; it was my friend Amy. I told her where I was and what was happening. Within two hours she was sitting next to me. She had packed up her baby daughter and headed up the motorway immediately. She didn't ask. She just came.

Amy's act reminded me of the Bible story about Ruth's bond with Naomi. When Naomi told Ruth to go back to her family, Ruth insisted on remaining at Naomi's side. We may be puzzled by Ruth's actions until we think about those dear to us who have not let us journey alone either.

Prayer: *Thank you, God, for companions who journey with us on difficult roads. Amen*

Thought for the day: We can be God's presence to those facing crisis.

Ruth Hetland (Colorado, US)

Good Morning, Moon

Read John 20:26–29

Jesus said to [Thomas], 'Have you believed because you have seen me? Blessed are those who have not seen and yet have come to believe.'
John 20:29 (NRSV)

Walking in my garden this morning, I was amazed to see the moon high in the sky, shining brightly in broad daylight. When I ran for my telescope and looked through it, I saw in crisp detail our moon's craters, plains and ridges.

It occurred to me then that seeing the moon in daytime is similar to being aware of God's presence. Just as we don't often see the moon in daytime, we don't always recognise God walking next to us. Some of those times when, like Thomas, we are finding it hard to believe in something—and Someone—we cannot see, God seems to send us a message. Perhaps this comes in the form of a helping hand from a stranger, or a friend remembering us with a letter or phone call. Or perhaps it is just a 'still, small voice' (1 Kings 19:12, KJV) speaking to us, encouraging and comforting us.

Our faith renewed, we are assured that God is with us—no matter what, no matter when. Buoyed by the times when we manage to witness and experience God's presence, we are better able to maintain our faith during difficult times. And our continuing faith in the unseen Lord can serve as a powerful witness to others.

Prayer: *Dear God, having faith is hard during times when you seem distant. Show us your presence in the people around us and as you speak to us through your word. Amen*

Thought for the day: Evidence of our unseen God can be seen in every day's events.

Tom Seymour (Maine, US)

Seek God First

Read 1 Kings 19:1–12
I call on the Lord in my distress, and he answers me.
Psalm 120:1 (NIV)

I've always been a worrier. However, I thought when I became a Christian that I would no longer worry or fear. When that didn't happen, I wondered what I was doing wrong. The story of Elijah gave me insight into the answer. Elijah relied on God day after day for survival, and he witnessed many miracles. He was fed by ravens, ate bread made from a nearly empty jug of oil and jar of flour, and saw a dead boy 'restored to life'.

Even though Elijah experienced all this, he was overwhelmed by fear when he heard of Jezebel's promise to kill him. Elijah depended on his own strength and eventually prayed for death. It wasn't until Elijah finally sought God that he was able to rest.

I was encouraged to see that fear and worry are common and normal emotions. I also realised that I should focus my effort not on eliminating emotion but on seeking God. God does not promise to deliver us from every difficulty, but we are promised that God will respond when we call, that God will give us the ability to get through the tough times. We can experience incomprehensible peace if we remember to seek God.

Prayer: *Lord, help us remember to look to you when we feel overwhelmed by circumstances around us. Amen*

Thought for the day: When I want to run away, instead I will run to God.

Link2Life: *Make a list of your worries and then burn or shred it as a sign of entrusting those concerns to God's care.*

Debbie S. Middlebrook (Georgia, US)

PRAYER FOCUS: THOSE WHO STRUGGLE WITH FEAR AND WORRY

The Older Brother

Read Luke 15:11–32

Let us therefore approach the throne of grace with boldness, so that we may receive mercy and find grace to help in time of need.
Hebrews 4:16 (NRSV)

My grandfather is a generous man. He has worked hard all his life; and his greatest joy is sharing what he has with others rather than using it all for himself. I have learned much about God's love through my grandfather's example.

Sometimes he has given money to members of our family when we have done nothing to deserve it. Occasionally, I hesitate to mention my needs to him. But he enjoys our requests; and within his means, he helps us.

When I read Luke 15:11–32, the story of the prodigal son, I think about the older son. He talks about not receiving something from his father even though he has not expressed his wishes. Like the father in the story and like my grandfather, God welcomes us to talk about our needs and desires.

But unlike my grandfather, God owns everything, God can do everything, and he knows everything. God welcomes our requests and feels joy in giving to us. We can ask God for all we need and trust that he will hear and respond in love.

Prayer: *Dear God, as a good father, you are generous and willing to give to us. May we trust in your love and your willingness to provide for all our needs. Amen*

Thought for the day: God wants to hear about our deepest needs.

Paola Mora (San Jose, Costa Rica)

God's Formations

Read Isaiah 43:14–21

The Lord says, 'See, I am doing a new thing! Now it springs up; do you perceive it? I am making a way in the desert and streams in the wasteland.'
Isaiah 43:19 (NIV)

As I gazed out the aeroplane window, I saw enormous cotton-wool clouds swirling around me. One large arrangement resembled a heart. 'Beautiful,' I mused. To my dismay the cloud began to break apart, chunks floating in each direction to mingle and form different shapes, until the heart was completely gone.

'If only things wouldn't change,' I sighed. Then realisation dawned. The clouds have to continue moving and changing to be used how and when God needs them. They are still clouds. Their purpose remains the same. But they have to break out of the form they've been in to create shade for new areas or to bring refreshing rain to different dry ground.

Without movement, clouds would not serve their purpose. We could say the same of God's people. God calls us to be a part of certain formations at certain points in our lives but also calls us to change and travel to meet new opportunities at other times. We don't have to be afraid to break with the old; the new design God is working on may be even better. The same One who holds together and directs the clouds above our heads certainly will care for us, so we can serve wherever God's call takes us.

Prayer: *Dear Father, help us not to fear the challenges life brings. Give us the courage to let go of the comfortable and familiar and step forward in faith. Amen*

Thought for the day: In every change God can work for the good.

Rosemarie Greenawalt (Alabama, US)

All Different

Read Psalm 107:1–15

Make a joyful noise unto the Lord, all ye lands. Serve the Lord with gladness: come before his presence with singing.
Psalm 100:1–2 (KJV)

I was born with a hole in the roof of my mouth that causes my speech to sound muffled and unclear. Throughout my life, I have complained to God because I am not like everyone else. I was bitter and unhappy for a long time; and my anger grew, especially a few years ago in my early teenage years—until I began noticing people around me.

I was shopping at a local supermarket when I approached a man who was moving slowly. His one arm and leg were completely paralysed. I looked more closely to see his face and found that he was laughing. Even without being able to use his arm and leg, he was happy. How could this be? I tried to think what life would be like if I did not have use of an arm and a leg.

Even though I have a problem speaking, I can still be thankful for my ability to talk. I learned that in life we often complain about our problems, only to find that other people have problems far worse than ours. While I was complaining, I was not looking to God and trusting God for who I am. Now I try to thank God for who I am, just as I am, though sometimes it is hard, and I pray for patience, joy and healing.

Prayer: *God, help us as we face our physical limitations. Protect us from discouraging thoughts, and replace frustration with joy. Amen*

Thought for the day: All of us imperfect people can thank God even in our imperfection.

Brent Jonathan Funk (Pennsylvania, US)

Immeasurable Value

Read Luke 11:5–13

I will be a Father to you, and you will be my sons and daughters, says the Lord Almighty.
2 Corinthians 6:18 (NIV)

We rose to greet a beautiful midsummer morning, and everything seemed just right. After gathering around the table for breakfast, we bowed our heads for the usual blessing. In a simple prayer, I expressed gratitude for refreshing sleep and the gift of a new day. Then, I said, 'And lead us through this day.'

Before I finished saying those words, they brought back vivid memories of childhood. In those days, I would place my little hand in the big hand of my father and follow him wherever he went. With no fear, I could go anywhere with him, for I had absolute confidence that he would guide me, protect me and get me to the proper destination. And I was never disappointed.

My experience with my father prepared me for something of immeasurable value. Very early I learned that we have a heavenly Father we can trust through all of life's circumstances. Even if we don't have trustworthy earthly fathers, we can place our hand in the hand of our eternal Father and follow in trust where God leads us.

Prayer: *Heavenly Father, many times we don't know where we ought to go. In those moments, we trust you to lead us. In Jesus' name we affirm it. Amen*

Thought for the day: Every day I can trust and follow where God leads me.

Howard Coop (Kentucky, US)

PRAYER FOCUS: CHILDREN WHOSE FATHERS ARE ABSENT

Reconciled

Read Romans 5:1–11

If, when we were God's enemies, we were reconciled to him through the death of his Son, how much more, having been reconciled, shall we be saved through his life!
Romans 5:10 (NIV)

Dan and I had been friends since college. We moved to different parts of the country after graduation but kept in touch. One evening during a phone conversation, Dan and I began to argue about our plans for a camping trip. The argument grew tense, we exchanged heated words, and we eventually hung up without apologising. For three months I did not call Dan, and he did not contact me.

During my devotional time one morning, I realised I was still angry with Dan. I knew that my anger would continue to grow if I did not face it and deal with it. I prayed and asked God to forgive me, and then I called Dan and apologised. He also apologised and asked for forgiveness. We talked for more than an hour, prayed for each other, and set up a weekend for our long-delayed camping trip.

All of us were once separated from God, but through Christ's death on the cross, we are now reconciled to God. We can rejoice in knowing that we are no longer God's enemies. Through the gift of Jesus, we have a relationship of peace with our Lord.

Prayer: *Thank you, Lord, for your grace in Jesus Christ, whose life, death, and resurrection reconcile us with you. Amen*

Thought for the day: How can I allow God to help me with troubled relationships?

Link2Life: *Call or write to someone with whom you have unresolved differences and begin to mend the rift between you.*

James C. Hendrix (Indiana, US)

New Lenses

Read Psalm 18:1–19

The Lord is my light and my salvation; whom shall I fear?
Psalm 27:1a (NRSV)

Some days ago I was wakened suddenly. The ground was shaking. It continued to move so violently and for so long that I got out of bed, realising that this was an earthquake. My husband and son did the same. We had never been in a situation like this, and all we could think to do was to cover ourselves and to huddle together. We were totally helpless before the power of nature, and we were deeply aware of our human frailty. I prayed fervently, asking God for protection and strength. Once the earthquake ended, I talked to my parents and friends to find out how they were doing.

Forgetting all that we felt during those moments will be difficult. When we feel nature's power in contrast to our human weakness, all that matters is life itself and the safety of our loved ones.

On these occasions, we appreciate life and realise what is truly valuable. Since that day, I have tried to spend more time with the people I love and to give God thanks for our life. Material things lose their value when we look at them through new lenses.

Prayer: *When natural disasters affect us, thank you, God, for teaching us what is valuable in life. Amen*

Thought for the day: What God teaches us through the hard times can guide us all the time.

Link2Life: *Looking at your calendar, consider your use of time and whether it reflects what is truly important to you.*

Giselle Fétis Navarrete (Araucanía, Chile)

PRAYER FOCUS: THOSE REBUILDING AFTER DISASTER

God's Eraser

Read Jonah 2:1–10
Jonah said, 'I called to the Lord out of my distress, and he answered me.'
Jonah 2:2 (NRSV)

A friend's granddaughter asked her to draw a picture of a horse with the granddaughter sitting on the horse. My friend, though an artist, said that she had never drawn a horse. Her granddaughter replied, 'All you need is a piece of paper, a pencil, and a good eraser.'

I believe that God has a good eraser. When I repent, God is continuously erasing what I do wrong. God knows my thoughts, my struggles and my hesitance to do good. I am imperfect, I know; but I keep striving to live as God wants me to. When I fail, God rescues me with an eraser ready and shows me the right path. I feel God's powerful love and grace.

Jonah cried out to God, and God gave him a second chance to do what he should have done in the first place. If we go in the wrong direction, we can ask God for another chance, as Jonah did. It is up to us to ask God to erase our sins and to restore our life.

Prayer: *Forgiving God, grant us your grace and understanding when we err, and guide us back to you. 'Our Father which art in heaven, Hallowed be thy name. Thy kingdom come. Thy will be done, as in heaven, so in earth. Give us day by day our daily bread. And forgive us our sins; for we also forgive every one that is indebted to us. And lead us not into temptation; but deliver us from evil.'**

Thought for the day: God's eraser has your name on it.

Anita J. McIntosh (North Carolina, US)

PRAYER FOCUS: SOMEONE WHO NEEDS A SECOND CHANCE
* Luke 11:2–4 (KJV)

Rules of the Road

Read 1 Peter 3:8–17

By this, everyone will know that you are my disciples, if you have love for one another.
John 13:35 (NRSV)

Recently I stopped in traffic behind a large truck. A sign prominently displayed on the truck's rear door asked the public to call a certain number if the truck driver was not obeying the rules of safe driving. Trucking companies displaying such signs surely have confidence in their drivers and in their training.

I began to wonder how my behaviour would change if Christians were required to wear a sign identifying us as Christians and requesting that our bad behaviour be reported. Would I be less likely to show frustration because of poor service? Would I be more patient while waiting in a queue at the bank or sitting in the doctor's office? Would I forgive more easily when others made comments that hurt my feelings? Perhaps I would offer to help a person in need more readily if I were wearing a sign that declares my faith.

All of us are challenged to follow God's direction in our day-to-day interactions. Whether or not our behaviour is noticed by anyone, we are always accountable to God.

Prayer: *Dear Lord, help us to turn to you for guidance daily, knowing that you care about every aspect of our lives. Amen*

Thought for the day: What will my actions reveal about my faith today?

Lois M. Baker (Kansas, US)

PRAYER FOCUS: PROFESSIONAL DRIVERS

Trusting God in School

Read Matthew 7:7–11

Ask, and it will be given to you; search, and you will find; knock, and the door will be opened for you.
Matthew 7:7 (NRSV)

I am ten years old and will be starting school again tomorrow. At Sunday school, I've learned that God has a special plan for me and that God will guide all of us and will help us reach our goals. God has given me good teachers who teach me and caring parents who support me. I know that I don't have to worry about school.

I've known all along that I need to work hard. Praying about my schoolwork also helps me. Near the end of last year, I realised that I need to trust God to help me; I need to picture myself succeeding and to anticipate that I'll do well. Jesus tells us, 'Ask, and it will be given to you' (Matthew 7:7). I believe that God will answer our prayers if what we ask is good for us. I did better than ever in school at the end of last year. School became more fun and less stressful.

By trusting in God, we can believe that good things will happen in the future and then watch them become real. I look forward to this school year as a chance to learn and grow alongside my friends and with help from good teachers, my parents and God.

Prayer: *Thank you, God, for always helping us, especially when our lives are stressful. Please help us to trust you always. Amen*

Thought for the day: Trusting in God is the most important step we can take toward success.

Link2Life: *Pray by name for children in your church as the new school year approaches.*

Will Buxton (California, US)

Holy Ground

Read Psalm 148
Indeed, the whole earth is mine.
Exodus 19:5 (NRSV)

Have you stood on holy ground? Perhaps you've stood inside St Paul's Cathedral in London, St Peter's Basilica in Rome, or the National Cathedral in Washington, DC. For some people, holy ground is a tiny white church in a quaint New England village or a church on the Gulf Coast that survived the hurricanes, a struggling town-centre church or a country chapel.

Moses walked over a large area of holy ground. So did the psalmist who proclaimed the marvel of God's power and creation. The apostle Peter stood on holy ground at the Mount of Transfiguration and when he carried forth the message of Jesus Christ. From birth to death to resurrection, Jesus walked on holy ground.

But holy ground is not limited to places where religious events have taken place; every place can constitute holy ground. Did astronauts walking on the moon perceive it as holy ground? After all, God has created this marvellous world, the land we walk on, the seas we sail, the skies above us.

Because all that surrounds us is holy, we cannot justify abuse of the land or pollution of streams, seas and skies. Nor can we account for the oppression of people or justify wars.

Perhaps God calls us to search our souls for how we can treasure and care for all that God has given us. It's up to humanity to live as if wherever we are is holy ground—because God is there.

Prayer: *Remind us, Lord, that you don't make rubbish; we do. Forgive us when we abuse your creation. Amen*

Thought for the day: All of God's creation can be holy ground.

Bruce A. Mitchell (Michigan, US)

PRAYER FOCUS: TO CARE FOR CREATION

131

Not Alone

Read Psalm 139:1–18
You hem me in, behind and before, and lay your hand upon me.
Psalm 139:5 (NRSV)

Today my daughter turned 20. She went to celebrate in a cafe with some friends. Other friends and acquaintances have been telephoning to wish her a happy birthday and have commented because I am at home by myself. I am glad for their congratulations but brush away their sympathy because I am not alone. The Lord is with me.

At the time my child was born, I never thought about God. In those days, I relied on my own strength and on the help of other people. Immediately after the birth, I was put in a ward alone, and everyone left. I lay on my own, helpless. No one came to help me, and I felt as though everyone had forgotten about me. I didn't even cry out to God. I knew nothing about faith. I knocked on the wall, but no one answered.

Today I see clearly that I was knocking in the wrong place. I am certain that if I had turned to God, I would have found help. Of course, God helped me anyway. Eventually one of the nurses appeared, but I can still remember the overwhelming loneliness.

Now I read Psalm 139 again and again, and I realise that whatever happens in my life, I have never been and will never be alone. God cares about me.

Prayer: *Thank you, Lord, for your constant care. Thank you that wherever we go, 'your hand shall lead [us], and your right hand shall hold [us] fast'. Amen (Psalm 139:10)*

Thought for the day: Because of God's faithfulness, we are never alone.

Galina Samson (Voronezh, Russia)

Litter Prayers

Read 1 Timothy 2:1–4

I urge that petitions, prayers, requests and thanksgivings be offered to God for all people.
1 Timothy 2:1 (GNB)

Walking is my exercise of choice, both physical and spiritual. While walking I can thank God for my health that allows me to take this walk, for a wonderful job that still leaves enough time each day for a walk, for the motivation to spend that time walking and for… litter.

Litter has changed my way of thinking. Not long ago, I saw litter only as an eyesore on the lovely green grass or freshly fallen snow. I saw only how it interrupted my walk because of my having to stop, pick it up and carry it to a litter bin. One day, after reaching out for a discarded beer can, I thought of people who struggle with alcohol addiction and prayed that God would heal them. As I picked up a fast-food wrapper, I prayed for people who don't have enough to eat or need to learn to eat more healthily. An empty nappy pack reminded me of young parents who may be struggling to hold their family together, and I prayed for God's strength to uphold them.

With each piece of litter, I became aware of new people and their needs. I have become grateful for the way God shows us where we can serve. I still wish those who drop litter would learn that God's beautiful world is not a rubbish dump. But I will continue to use their litter as reminders to pray for them and others.

Prayer: *Keeper of our souls, thank you for knowing us intimately and for speaking to us in ways you know we will hear. Amen*

Thought for the day: Our attitude determines whether we see litter or incentives to pray.

Pat Herring (Ohio, US)

Small Group Questions

Wednesday 4 May

1. How would you define 'the timely word'? What is required to develop a 'mastery of the timely word'?

2. What passages from the Bible describe or directly say how God feels about us as divine creations?

3. Compare God's love to the love of a parent or grandparent, sibling or spouse. How are they the same? How are they different?

4. Read aloud Proverbs 10:19. What do you think that proverb means? How do these words apply to this meditation? What else does the Bible say about our speaking to others?

5. 1 John 3:1 says that God lavishes love on us. When have you felt God's love lavished on you? In general, what helps you to feel assured that you are loved?

6. What messages of love do you want to leave with those you love before your life ends? What holds you back from offering those messages now?

Wednesday 11 May

1. How important is it for the pastor of a church to be known in the community? Give reasons for your answer.

2. Did your parents live what they taught you? How did this affect you? In what ways are consistency of words and actions more important for a Christian than for a non-believer?

3. Read aloud Matthew 11:3–5. How are these statements true of your faith community? Should they be true of all Christian groups?

4. How can we ensure that the credit for our good deeds and reputation goes to God?

5. Do your neighbours and colleagues know that you are a Christian? If so, why? If not, why not? Should they? Should all our neighbours know that we're believers?

6. Looking back over the last 24 hours, what have you 'said' about Christ through your words and actions?

Wednesday 18 May

1. What unexpected event has taken away your certainty and challenged your faith? What helped you to survive the challenges?

2. What can we do to help people who are facing great losses?

3. What scripture passages have helped you in times of uncertainty? When if ever is quoting scripture not a good idea?

4. This writer was not cured physically but seems whole spiritually. What is the difference between being healed and being whole? Which is more common?

5. Does your church have a plan for helping members who face sudden difficulties? If so, what is it? How might such a plan be a good idea? What could you do to promote having such a plan?

6. Recount a time when you were at your lowest. Did you find strength and comfort? What/who was the source? How can we come to see God as that ultimate source?

7. What does the Bible say about facing the events of tomorrow? How does God comfort us in these verses/passages?

Wednesday 25 May

1. Do you have a clear sense of your purpose in life? If so, how did you come to it? What are the advantages of knowing and being held accountable for living our purpose?

2. What small things or 'few things' has God entrusted to your care? How have you seen God increase your responsibility over time?

3. What do Old Testament books such as Ecclesiastes, Psalms and Proverbs have to say about our purpose in life? How do they apply to our modern lives?

4. Have you ever had the sense that God suddenly included a new verse in a familiar Bible passage? Recount a time when a scripture passage or verse took on new meaning for you.

5. When has dissatisfaction led you into greater devotion to God?

6. How might we find reward in what we consider insignificant labour? What does God see in our ordinary acts of obedience?

Wednesday 1 June

1. Have you asked others to pray for you? If so, when was the last time, and what was your concern? How have those prayers been answered?

2. How do you respond to the image of prayer as hard work? What feelings and thoughts are evoked by that image?

3. Describe something you have 'laboured fervently' for. How might you apply the same zeal to praying for others?

4. 1 Thessalonians 5:16–18 tells us to 'pray without ceasing'. What do you think this means for busy, real life?

5. Do you believe God cares about how we pray or how much we pray? What does God want for us regarding prayer?

6. Does this meditation make you want to pray more or less? Why?

7. What is your favourite Bible story or passage about prayer, and why?

Wednesday 8 June

1. Who is/are the best neighbour/s you've ever had, and why so? How have they affected you?

2. What old habits and feelings still appear in your actions even though you've asked God for help to change? How do you feel about yourself when they do? How do you think God feels about you at such times?

3. 'Forgive and forget.' When and why is that possible? Impossible? When should we resolve not to forget?

4. Are we obligated to forgive if someone does not repent or ask us for forgiveness? Is God? What scripture passages support your answers?

5. In what ways might conscience and good manners parallel God's ethics? How and why do the Bible's statements about what is right differ from human principles?

6. Is forgiveness more essential for the one forgiving or the one being forgiven? Why?

Wednesday 15 June

1. What good 'seedlings' have cropped up for you lately? Had you noticed them before that question? What does your answer say about daily occurrences and attitudes?

2. When you must choose between two equally good opportunities to serve, how do you decide which to say yes to and which to say no to? How and why can/should we say no to requests that don't fit our spiritual gifts?

3. How would you define 'a balanced life'? Does the Bible tell us to live a balanced life and show us how? Cite verses or scripture stories to support your answer.

4. What are the three most important acts you do each week? Why do you consider them so? How does faith help us set priorities and guide us in addressing them?

5. Recount a time or situation when following Christ's admonition in Matthew 6:33 was/is easy and one in which it was/is hard.

6. How does the story of Mary and Martha relate to this meditation (Luke 10:38–42)?

Wednesday 22 June

1. Do you agree with this writer's philosophy about giving? Why or why not?

2. Do we have no responsibility about how others use what we give them? What about the toys we give to children or money we lend? Should we give these and then forget about the giving?

3. What limits do you place on your giving? Why?

4. Do you always respond the same way to someone asking for a handout, or does your response vary with the situation?

5. In what areas of your life do you have more than you need? How do you share this abundance in the name of Christ?

6. What Bible passages other than those mentioned in today's meditation do you find instructive for your giving? How has giving changed you?

Wednesday 29 June

1. How has prayer helped you in some emergency?

2. Who has taught you most about praying? What books, retreats or teachers have changed the way you pray? How has praying changed you?

3. What do people mean when they contrast 'personal relationship with God' and dutiful or learned faith? Do you feel that you have such a personal relationship? Why or why not?

4. How could 'dutiful religion' be important to our faith? How could 'dutiful religion' be important to a growing relationship with God?

5. What would you define as an 'exciting prayer'? How often do you see your prayers this way?

6. Where and how have you undergone 'spiritual surgery' in recent years? Where do you still need help and growth?

Wednesday 6 July

1. What was your favourite childhood 'secret place' to hide and think? What most often sent you there? What is your 'secret place' now, and what does it do for you?

2. What are some apparently innocent activities that can become 'briar patches'? How can we prepare to cope with them? What 'briar patches' have you found yourself in lately?

3. How is sin like a briar patch? How is the image of being in a briar patch inadequate for describing what sin is and does?

4. Do you believe that God is always willing to swoop in and rescue us as the dad in this meditation did? Is it okay to ask God to rescue us when we get ourselves into a mess? Why or why not? Have you ever had the sense that God is rescuing you?

5. What are the limits of comparing God's work to this father's actions? What are the limits of comparing God to a father in general?

6. What is your most entangling sin (Hebrews 12:1, NIV)—the sin that draws you the most? What has helped you most in battling that sin?

7. What is required of us to avoid committing sin in our life? How does God set us free from sin?

Wednesday 13 July

1. If your pastor asked you to lead a Bible study, how would you respond? Why?

2. Not 'enough help, enough money, enough time, or enough talent'. Which do you use most often as an excuse? Which do you use most often in the church?

3. How is 'I don't have time' always untrue to some extent? Why do some people seem to have more time than others even though we all get exactly 24 hours each day?

4. Do you prefer the role of follower or of leader? Why?

5. What is your church doing to feed the hungry? What are you doing?

6. What talent, ability or skill would the people in your group be surprised to learn that you have? Why is it a secret?

7. When have you faced a challenge that seemed impossible but met it? How do we tap into God's power when we find ourselves in such situations?

8. When have you been surprised to see/witness 'the miraculous power of the Holy Spirit'? How is God working through you to help others?

Wednesday 20 July

1. What is the most fun you've had volunteering? Why was it fun? What has been the most challenging volunteer work you've done, and why?

2. How does your church community serve housebound people? Do you reach out to those in the greater community as well? If so, how? If not, why not?

3. What ministry areas have drawn your participation and/or support? Do you give them money or time or both? Generally, which do you prefer to give? Why?

4. When has someone helped you with something you could not do by yourself? Did this experience encourage you to offer your help to another? Why or why not?

5. Do you plan to be an organ donor? If not, why not? If so, do you carry a donor card, and have you made known your wishes about this?

6. In what areas of your life are you most blessed? How can you use these gifts for God's purposes?

Wednesday 27 July

1. Talk about the last time you got lost. How did you respond? What is your typical reaction in such situations? Is that reaction a positive Christian witness to others?

2. Typically, do you pray before you begin a big project or plan a trip?

3. What do you think are the most important 'direction signs' in the Bible? What has happened to you when you failed to follow them?

4. What Bible verse has come to mind in some difficult situation and helped you decide what to do or settled your emotions? Why and how did it help you?

5. Are you a planner, or do you prefer to 'take life as it comes'? If the former, in what areas do you find it hardest to give up control to God? If the latter, in what ways can you identify with what this writer is saying?

6. What earthly 'guides' compete with God? When have you followed 'guides' who led you the wrong way? What did this experience/these experiences teach you?

7. For what situation in your life are you searching for God's guidance right now? How do you seek God's guidance? If you're not asking for God's guidance, why not?

8. Reread the 'Thought for the Day'. Why would we rely on God to 'handle our baggage' as an afterthought rather than relying on God for guidance to begin with?

Wednesday 3 August

1. How have current economic conditions affected you? What changes have you made because of economic pressures, if any?

2. Talking about money is generally a taboo in our culture. Did the last question cause you discomfort inwardly? Should Christians be able to talk about money and financial needs/pressures more easily than non-believers? Why or why not?

3. How would your congregation respond to a man such as Shaun describes?

4. How can Christ's followers keep from wanting to 'lay up treasures on earth' when the world emphasises money and power as measures of success?

5. How is your church involved in ministry to and with homeless people? If you are involved, why? What do you get out of it? If not, what holds you back?

6. If you made a list of your 'earthly treasures' and another list of your heavenly treasures, how would they differ in length and content?

7. What earthly treasures attract you the most? Are they inherently bad? When can something good become bad for us?

8. Is it okay to give of your time but not your money—or the other way around? When/how?

Wednesday 10 August

1. How did you respond to this man's statements that he was simultaneously a church-going believer and an alcoholic? Did he surprise or shock you? Why or why not?

2. If you think and speak of alcoholism as a sin rather than an illness, why? If you think of it as an illness rather than a sin, why?

3. Which is harder for you to reconcile with Christian belief: this man's drinking or his rage? Why?

4. What 'addictions' do we accept in believers in ways that we do not accept alcoholism? Why do some addictions seem more acceptable than others?

5. When has your Christian example been less than shining? Which fruit of the spirit would have made a difference if you'd shown it? What can we do to increase our 'fruit harvest'?

6. Is 'self control' the only fruit of the Spirit that could help with addiction? Why or why not? Which other 'fruits' might be relative to addiction? How so?

7. In what ways are all of us 'a contradiction of light and darkness'? Given this, how can anyone be an example of a Christian?

8. Looking back on your life, how has God moved you from darkness to light?

Wednesday 17 August

1. Do you have a friend like Amy? If so, what illustrates this person's love and commitment to you? For whom have you been a friend like Amy?

2. Does a friend have to be a Christian to be considered a gift from God? Why or why not?

3. Who do you know who is watching at the bedside of a loved one who is seriously ill? What have you done and can you do to offer support? Does your congregation do this well for its members? Does your congregation do it for non-members?

4. What do you suppose made Ruth willing to leave her family and home country to travel with Naomi into an uncertain future?

5. Have you ever taken a risky step like Ruth's, breaking dramatically with what was expected of you? If so, why? If not, what could you need to be able to do so?

6. What would you list as your greatest losses? Why would these make the list?

7. What factors determine how well people recover from a loss? Are there some losses we never recover from? Should Christians face loss differently from non-believers?

Wednesday 24 August

1. How did you come to know about and read *The Upper Room*? Did you begin by reading sporadically? If so, why and when did you begin to read more regularly?

2. What meditation or writer has been most memorable to you in the time you've been reading this magazine, and why? In what situations does this person or writing come to mind?

3. How does your day-to-day behaviour model the life and love of Christ to others?

4. For whom have you been a spiritual encourager/nagger? Does anything in this meditation cause you to think you should change your approach, and if so, how?

5. Describe one or two of your Christian mentors. Did you choose them for this role? What qualifies them for it? Should we consciously seek spiritual mentors?

6. Do you think it is better to emulate famous strangers or people we know personally? Why? What are good reasons for looking to people as examples?

7. In addition to prayer, worship and Bible study, what activities, practices or routines make you feel closer to God? Could these be considered spiritual disciplines too? How so?

Wednesday 31 August

1. For what 'ordinary blessings' are you grateful today? What blessings do we often fail to notice or to name as blessings?

2. Do you exercise regularly? If so, what is your favourite form of exercise? How could regular exercise be an act of discipleship?

3. What small act of faithfulness always gets your attention when you see others do it? Why does this act matter to you?

4. What have you seen people do today that is not kind to the environment? What does your community of faith do to help care for our world? Should concern for Earth be a part of our discipleship? Why?

5. Look around you. What groups of people or concerns do you see that we might pray for?

6. In what ways other than the ones Pat Herring mentions can we use everyday activities and objects as aids to our praying?

7. What kind of neighbour are you? What kind of neighbour would you like to be?

8. Do your prayers tend to be general or specific and detailed—or both? Explain. What Bible story or verse about prayer most challenges you? Why?

Bible Reading Resources Pack

A pack of resources and ideas to help to promote Bible reading in your church is available from BRF. The pack, which will be of use at any time during the year (but especially for Bible Sunday in October), includes sample readings from BRF's Bible reading notes and The People's Bible Commentary, a sermon outline, an all-age sketch, a children's activity, information about BRF's ministry and much more.

Unless you specify the month in which you would like the pack sent, we will send it immediately on receipt of your order. We greatly appreciate your donations towards the cost of producing the pack (without them we would not be able to make the pack available) and we welcome your comments about the contents of the pack and your ideas for future ones.

This coupon should be sent to:
BRF, 15 The Chambers, Vineyard, Abingdon OX14 3FE

Name...

Address ....

....Postcode....................................

Telephone ....

Email...

Please send me....................................Bible Reading Resources Pack(s).

Please send the pack now/ in ....(month).

I enclose a donation for £.................... towards the cost of the pack.

BRF is a Registered Charity

Subscriptions

The Upper Room is published in January, May and September.

Individual subscriptions

The subscription rate for orders for 4 or fewer copies includes postage and packing: THE UPPER ROOM annual individual subscription   £13.80

Church subscriptions

Orders for 5 copies or more, sent to ONE address, are post free:
THE UPPER ROOM annual church subscription   £10.80

Please do not send payment with order for a church subscription. We will send an invoice with your first order.

Please note that the annual billing period for church subscriptions runs from 1 May to 30 April.

Copies of the notes may also be obtained from Christian bookshops.

Single copies of *The Upper Room* will cost £3.60. Prices valid until 30 April 2012.

Individual Subscriptions

☐ I would like to take out a subscription myself (complete your name and address details only once)

☐ I would like to give a gift subscription (please complete both name and address sections below)

Your name...

Your address...

....Postcode...

Gift subscription name..

Gift subscription address..

....Postcode...

Gift message (20 words max)..

....

Please send *The Upper Room* beginning with the September 2011 / January 2012 / May 2012 issue: (delete as applicable)

THE UPPER ROOM ☐ £13.80

Please complete the payment details below and send, with appropriate payment, to: BRF, 15 The Chambers, Vineyard, Abingdon OX14 3FE

Total enclosed £.......... (cheques should be made payable to 'BRF')

Payment by ☐ cheque ☐ postal order ☐ Visa ☐ Mastercard ☐ Switch

Card no:																			

Expires:				Security code:			

Issue no (Switch): ☐☐☐☐

Signature (essential if paying by credit/Switch card) ....

☐ Please do not send me further information about BRF publications

☐ Please send me a Bible reading resources pack to encourage Bible reading in my church

BRF is a Registered Charity

UR0211

148

Church Subscriptions

☐ Please send me ...... copies of *The Upper Room* September 2011 / January 2012 / May 2012 issue (delete as applicable)

Name...

Address ....

....Postcode.......................................

Telephone ....

Email...

Please send this completed form to:
BRF, 15 The Chambers, Vineyard, Abingdon OX14 3FE

Please do not send payment with this order. We will send an invoice with your first order.

Christian bookshops: All good Christian bookshops stock BRF publications. For your nearest stockist, please contact BRF.

Telephone: The BRF office is open between 09.15 and 17.30. To place your order, telephone 01865 319700; fax 01865 319701.

Web: Visit www.brf.org.uk

☐ Please send me a Bible reading resources pack to encourage Bible reading in my church

BRF is a Registered Charity

UR0211

Mustard Seed Shavings

Mountain-moving for beginners

Steve Tilley

Not read any Christian book before but want to give it a go? Maybe, just maybe, this will help.

Taken a first step of faith—or a first step in taking faith more seriously—but don't quite know what to do next? Possibly you are holding something useful.

Mustard Seed Shavings offers a gentle introduction to Christian lifestyle, using the Ten Commandments as a framework. It tries to show what following Jesus means in practice today. Hopefully it reads more like receiving a present than being given a rule-book.

Each chapter ends with a pause for thought, a couple of discussion questions and a brief prayer. So, not the last word or the tiny details, but perhaps a nice place to begin.

ISBN 978 1 84101 828 7   £5.99

To order a copy of this book, please turn to the order form on page 157.

Word and Spirit

The vital partnership in Christian leadership

Will Donaldson

The Bible—the Word of God—and the Spirit of God are inextricably bound together, as the story of God's working throughout history reveals. The Word tells of God's unfolding purposes for the salvation of his world, and trains us in godly living. The Spirit inspires and illumines the text and fills us with power and gifts for ministry and mission. Sadly, 'Word' and 'Spirit' have become increasingly identified with divergent parts of the Church, impoverishing our witness and weakening the body of Christ.

This book calls Christians to focus on what unites rather than divides, and to come together in a celebration of both Word and Spirit to build each other up and further the sharing of the gospel. It not only traces the shaping of this 'vital partnership' through Christian history, but explores their shared importance in key areas of church leadership and ministry.

ISBN 978 1 84101 825 6   £8.99

To order a copy of this book, please turn to the order form on page 157.

Creative Mission

Over 50 ideas for special days, celebrations, festivals, community-based projects and seasonal activities

Rona Orme

Creative Mission sets out to demonstrate that mission is fun, practical, easy-to-do and, above all, possible. The book contains a wealth of ideas to help churches, large and small, urban and rural, to connect with people who have occasional contact with the church, as well as suggestions for the church family to join in community events.

Many of the ideas are for families, children and adults, to enjoy together or alongside one another. Some ideas can be used within worship; others are for social events, fundraising activities, campaigns for justice across the world or RE and assemblies in schools. All will appeal to children as well as adults, but many can also be used if there are few or no children in the church family.

The ideas are arranged in four sections to fit with the seasons of the year. Some follow the church calendar; others link with secular high points in the year such as Valentine's Day, Red Nose Day, Father's Day and 'Back to School'.

The suggestions are offered for both traditional churches and Fresh Expressions of church to select those that will work best for them and the community they serve.

ISBN 978 1 84101 806 5   £8.99

To order a copy of this book, please turn to the order form on page 157.

Time for Reflection

Meditations to use through the year

Ann Persson

It is not easy to switch from activity to stillness, from noise to silence, from achieving to letting go, from doing to being in the presence of God. This book of biblically rooted meditations provides accessible and practical routes to exploring prayer as that way of being in God's presence, letting the sediment of our lives settle so that we may have a true reflection of ourselves and of God within us.

Loosely based around the seasons of the Church year and also drawing inspiration from the seasons of nature, the meditations range from short 'spaces for grace' to longer exercises that can form the basis for a personal quiet day or retreat.

ISBN 978 1 84101 876 8   £8.99
To order a copy of this book, please turn to the order form on page 157.

Pilgrimage

The journey to remembering our story

Andrew Jones

The age-old practice of pilgrimage is more popular than it has been for centuries. At a time when the Church seems increasingly exiled and estranged from our culture, more and more people are treading the ancient pilgrim routes, whether they are committed Christians, spiritual seekers or simply curious. The renewal of faith that they find on their journey often outweighs what happens in many churches.

Andrew Jones shows how pilgrimage can awaken those at all stages of belief to remembering the story of God's creating and redeeming work in history, which tells us who we are, where we have come from and where we are going. The act of remembering it not only offers a life-transforming way out of exile but points to the way home, to the place where we can live authentic and balanced lives. The book concludes with a focus on eight popular places of pilgrimage in the British Isles, drawing lessons from their history and spiritual heritage that can encourage and inspire us on our own faith journeys.

ISBN 978 1 84101 834 8   £8.99

To order a copy of this book, please turn to the order form on page 157.

Sharing Faith the Jesus Way

Jim Currin

Faith is personal, but it is not private. We are Christians today because other people shared their faith in the past. We might think the good news mainly came to us through Peter, Paul and the other great preachers that have followed since. In fact, the gospel travelled down the centuries in a variety of ways—chiefly through ordinary Christians doing ordinary things made extraordinary by the Holy Spirit. We are part of a 2000-year-old chain.

This book is written for all those who feel they cannot share their faith, or have never read about doing it before now. Together we shall explore principles linked to how Jesus shared the good news: on the road, in the home, on a lake or up a mountain. We shall read the Gospels and follow his example, to make it possible, natural and a positive experience as we pray. Each chapter includes practical exercises to explore with a friend or wider group.

ISBN 978 1 84101 862 1 £6.99
To order a copy of this book, please turn to the order form on page 157.

ORDERFORM

REF	TITLE	PRICE	QTY	TOTAL
828 7	Mustard Seed Shavings	£5.99		
825 6	Word and Spirit	£8.99		
806 5	Creative Mission	£8.99		
876 8	Time for Reflection	£8.99		
834 8	Pilgrimage	£8.99		
862 1	Sharing Faith the Jesus Way	£6.99		

POSTAGE AND PACKING CHARGES

Order value	UK	Europe	Surface	Air Mail
£7.00 & under	£1.25	£3.00	£3.50	£5.50
£7.10–£30.00	£2.25	£5.50	£6.50	£10.00
Over £30.00	FREE	prices on request		

Postage and packing	
Donation	
TOTAL	

Name _____ Account Number _____

Address _____

_____ Postcode _____

Telephone Number_____

Email _____

Payment by: ❑ Cheque ❑ Mastercard ❑ Visa ❑ Postal Order ❑ Maestro

Card no ▢▢▢▢ ▢▢▢▢ ▢▢▢▢ ▢▢▢▢ ▢▢▢▢ ▢▢▢

Valid from ▢▢▢▢ Expires ▢▢▢▢ Issue no. ▢▢▢

Security code* ▢▢▢ *Last 3 digits on the reverse of the card.
ESSENTIAL IN ORDER TO PROCESS YOUR ORDER

Shaded boxes for Maestro use only

Signature _____ Date _____

All orders must be accompanied by the appropriate payment.

Please send your completed order form to:
BRF, 15 The Chambers, Vineyard, Abingdon OX14 3FE
Tel. 01865 319700 / Fax. 01865 319701 Email: enquiries@brf.org.uk

❑ Please send me further information about BRF publications.

Available from your local Christian bookshop.

BRF is a Registered Charity

About
brf:

BRF is a registered charity and also a limited company, and has been in existence since 1922. Through all that we do—producing resources, providing training, working face-to-face with adults and children, and via the web—we work to resource individuals and church communities in their Christian discipleship through the Bible, prayer and worship.

Our Barnabas children's team works with primary schools and churches to help children under 11, and the adults who work with them, to explore Christianity creatively and to bring the Bible alive.

To find out more about BRF and its core activities and ministries, visit:

www.brf.org.uk
www.brfonline.org.uk
www.barnabasinschools.org.uk
www.barnabasinchurches.org.uk
www.messychurch.org.uk
www.foundations21.org.uk

If you have any questions about BRF and our work, please email us at

enquiries@brf.org.uk